Europa, Europa

EUROPA, EUROPA

Solomon Perel

Translated from the German by
Margot Bettauer Dembo

Published in association with the
United States Holocaust Memorial Museum

JOHN WILEY & SONS, INC.

New York • Chichester • Weinheim • Brisbane • Singapore • Toronto

This book is printed on acid-free paper. ♾

English language translation copyright © 1997 by John Wiley & Sons, Inc. All rights reserved.

Originally published in French in 1990 as *Europa, Europa* copyright © 1990 by Éditions Ramsay

German edition published in 1992 as *Ich war Hitlerjunge Salomon* copyright © 1992 by Nicolaische Verlagsbuchhandlung Beuermann GmbH and Autorenagentur lansk mehr, both Berlin

Epilogue originally published in 1993 copyright © 1993 by Wilhelm Heyne Verlag GmbH & Co. KG, München

Published by John Wiley & Sons, Inc.
Published simultaneously in Canada.

Library of Congress Cataloging-in-Publication Data

Perel, Shlomo
    [Kor 'im li Shelomoh Perel. English]
    Europa, Europa / Solomon Perel ; translated from the German by Margot Bettauer Dembo.
      p.   cm.
    ISBN 0-471-17218-9 (cloth : alk. paper)
    ISBN 0-471-28364-9 (paper : alk. paper)
    1. Holocaust, Jewish (1939–1945)—Personal narratives. 2. Perel, Shlomo, 1925– 3. Hitler-Jugend—Biography. I. Dembo, Margot Bettauer. II. Title.
D804.3.P46513   1997
940.53'18—dc21   96-46844

Dedicated

to the memory of my mother, Rebecca,

my father, Azriel,

and my sister, Bertha,

who were victims of the Holocaust.

And to the memory of my brother, Isaac,

who died while I was writing this account.

Contents

PREFACE

My Holocaust experiences reported here are true. These events actually happened to me. This story recounts the feelings and thoughts that have refused to leave me since my youth, spent in fear and persecution in the middle of beleaguered and tragic Europe under the terror of German occupation.

Just as one single faithfully recounted testimony of the horror of the Holocaust is the most convincing way to make people remember the past, so too is it a warning for the future. Therefore, I am especially pleased with the initiative of the United States Holocaust Memorial Museum and John Wiley and Sons in bringing out this particular edition, making available in the English language this unique examination of a life lived in the Nazi state. At the same time my thanks and acknowledgements go to the sponsoring editor, Ms. Hana Lane, and to the translator, Margot Dembo. I offer, too, my especial appreciation to my literary agent, Edwin D. Rosenberger; to Benton Arnovitz, Director of Academic Publications at the Museum; and to Henry Wimpfheimer, Esq.

With this English-language edition goes my wish that readers will find it interesting, that it will reach the depths of the souls of young people, and that it will register as a call for tolerance and human dignity.

Solomon Perel
Givatayim, Israel

PROLOGUE

I have often been asked why I never published my story. Unfortunately, until now I have found it impossible to provide a clear and satisfying answer. Probably I didn't want to be reminded of the past and the tragic events connected with it. In fact, for many years I tried hard to suppress and forget what happened. My daily routine forced me to put the subject aside and only rarely was there opportunity to seriously reflect. The time was just not ripe.

Sometimes I felt the urge to describe my adventures, but always there were questions that virtually paralyzed me: Did I really have the right to compare myself with survivors of the Holocaust? To consider myself part of their story? To place my memories on the same level as theirs? Did I have the right to compare myself with the resistance fighters, the inmates of concentration camps and ghettos, and with those who hid in forests, bunkers, and monasteries? They were heroes and heroines. Their suffering had brought them to the edge of human endurance. And yet with their last ounce of strength they had succeeded in retaining their Jewish identity, their humanity.

I, on the other hand, had gone about among the Nazis at this same time, unmolested, had worn their uniform that included a swastika on my cap, and had yelled *"Heil Hitler!"* as though I really identified with their criminal ideology and their barbaric goals.

What message did I have to pass on? Would people even believe my story? Would they try to understand it? And if I did put it all down on paper, would I be prepared to endure the loneliness and the isolation that accompany the writing of such a long account, as well as all the nightmares, pangs of conscience, and self-doubts that would emerge to torment me?

I thought about these questions for more than forty years—until I came to the conclusion that I had no other choice. Because as time went by I realized that I could no longer suppress the trauma, could no longer live with this spiritual incubus. To free myself of it I had to write it all down—to get it off my chest.

I promised myself, and I promise you, the reader, to stick to the truth from beginning to end. The barriers are down . . . and I'm ready to awaken painful memories, the memories of my *Shoah.*

You may well recall the famous director Elia Kazan's renowned 1960s book and film entitled *America, America.* In them he recounts Voltaire's classic story of Candide, a sailor who finds himself cast ashore among cannibals in South America. After many dangerous adventures he survives healthy and intact.

In my book you will see that I also perceived myself as having been cast among cannibals for whom I would have been an easy victim. Agnieska Holland, the director of the film based upon my experiences, viewed me as the Candide of the twentieth century. But my adventures had been in Europe, not America; hence the title *Europa, Europa.*

1

FLIGHT TO THE EAST

I was born on April 21, 1925, in Peine, a town near Brunswick in Germany.

My parents had moved to Germany in 1918 shortly after the October Revolution broke out in Russia. In those days the Weimar Republic was quite willing to admit Jew: were four children in our family. My oldest broth(was sixteen years old when I was born, David wa: and my sister, Bertha, nine.

To support the family, my parents opened a sh.. on the main street, Breite Strasse, shortly after their arrival in Peine. Our German neighbors at that time were not hostile to us, but the old established Jews, who had been in Germany for generations, gave us a cool reception.

They looked down on us East European Jews. Occasionally someone in my family would complain about this at home, but it didn't bother me much. How was I, who never could understand the difference between a Jew and a non-Jew, supposed to grasp the difference between one Jew and another Jew?

Peine was not a modern city, but gradually technological progress was felt there too. I remember how delighted we children were to see the first automobiles. They looked like carriages without horses, and each had a huge horn next to the steering wheel. We would run after them, eager to squeeze the "black pear" to make it honk and honk. . . .

Not a cloud marred the happiness of my childhood. We had no forebodings of the fateful events to come. And yet, in the dark years ahead, fifty million people of many lands were to lose their lives, and the *Shoah*, the systematically planned murder of the European Jews, would profoundly convulse our history.

On January 30, 1933, the National Socialist party under its leader Adolf Hitler came to power in Germany.

This marked the beginning of a black-brown dance of death: black and brown like the Nazi party uniforms, blood-red like that associated with various emblems and regalia of the SS, SA, and Hitler Youth.

As early as 1921, in order to protect the National Socialist party, which he was in the process of expanding, Hitler had created the SA, the *Sturmabteilung*, or Storm Troopers. Those who joined the SA were mainly former soldiers, men who could no longer fit into society. Germany's defeat in the First World War had embittered them. The SA was supposed to create unrest, break up meetings of opposition parties, and at the same time make sure that Nazi party meetings went off smoothly. They spread fear and terror and thus helped give the appearance that the Weimar Republic, which they were trying to undermine, was powerless. With Hitler and his friends firmly in the saddle, the dirty work was left to the SA: the persecution and liquidation of the Jews and all opponents of the regime.

The SS, *Schutzstaffel*, Protective Squad or Guard Detachment, was created in 1923. In disarray after the failed Munich putsch, it was reestablished in 1925. Although subordinate to the SA, the SS, acting as bodyguards for Hitler, considered themselves independent. In 1934 they were given that status officially, and reported directly to the Führer. Heinrich Himmler was chief of the SS. His fiefdom also included the *Gestapo*, the Secret State Police; the *Sicherheitsdienst* (SD), the Security Service that was in charge of the concentration camps; and the *Einsatzkommandos*, battalion-sized mobile units that operated in the occupied territories and killed men, women, and children there.

The *Hitlerjugend* (HJ), or Hitler Youth, was founded in 1926. This organization participated actively in street fights, demonstrations, and all events and functions intended to demonstrate the superiority of the Nazi terror. Its "elite" members were selected for SS service on the basis of their height, Nordic appearance, and pure Aryan bloodline.

Meanwhile, life in Peine went on even as the situation was growing rapidly more dismal. But it hardly affected us children. Nothing could keep us from racing wildly through the town playing our games. No doubt I wasn't mature enough to recognize the dangers that lay ahead, especially since my father, like so many others, thought that the "crazy guy" couldn't last very long and wouldn't stay in power more than eighty days. Like cries in the wilderness, the few warnings that were raised went unheeded.

Two years later, in 1935, I had my first personal encounter with persecution: in accordance with the Nuremberg racial laws, I was expelled from school. Everyday life became more and more difficult and dangerous. Several times my father was picked up and forced to scrub the streets or collect garbage. The SA boycotted Jewish businesses, smashed their shop windows, and committed other illegal acts.

Like a vise, the terror that threatened our existence was tightening its grip daily. At this point my family decided to leave Germany without further delay.

In great haste, we were forced to sell most of our property for pitifully little money. Practically penniless, we emigrated to Poland and settled in Lodz. At first we stayed with my mother's younger sister, Aunt Clara Wachsmann.

It wasn't easy to get used to life in a new country. The language as well as the mind-set in Poland were very different from what we had known before. Homesick for Germany, where I had been so happy as a child, I was profoundly shaken by this sudden and cruel uprooting. I simply couldn't come to terms with all these changes.

I had become a refugee child. And to make matters worse, I found out there was no sympathy here for refugees. The loud scornful snickering of the local Jewish kids who mocked the *Yeke Putz mit a Top Kawe* [the German Jewish loser with a pot of coffee]* hurt me and increased my bewilderment. I was less and less able to cope with the trials that were part of settling down.

Nevertheless, life continued, and gradually the terrible tensions I had been experiencing lessened and disappeared. I decided I just had to pull myself together, and it helped to be attending public school again. I learned to speak Polish with amazing speed.

Gradually a new way of life emerged. Studying Polish history—learning about the great men of Poland and their constant fight for national independence and against partition and foreign domination—gave me a greater liking for Poland. Little by little I had a vague feeling that it could be my second homeland.

Three years passed. The 1939 school year was drawing to a close. I had successfully completed elementary school, and my basic public school education was now finished. Af-

---

* Just as many German Jews thought their Eastern cousins shabby and uncultured, many East European Jews saw German Jews as arrogant emulators of gentile Germans, and Germans were thought to drink too much coffee.

With my elementary school seventh-grade class, Lodz, 1939. I'm in the second row, second from the left.

ter the summer vacation I was to transfer to the Jewish high school in Lodz.

I still remember the words of the valedictory song we sang with tears in our eyes, before we all went our separate ways:

Life slips by so quickly,
Time flows past like a stream.
In a year, a day, a moment
We'll no longer be together,
And deep in our hearts
Only sadness, regret, and yearning shall remain.

We had no inkling that not only would we no longer be together, but many of us soon would no longer even *be*.

September 1, 1939. Hitler's armies invaded Poland, dragging much of humanity into World War II.

We listened that day to Hitler's menacing speech on the radio as well as the reply by the Polish army chief of staff, Marshal Ridz Szmígly, who declared that Poland would fight courageously and would not hand over an inch of its territory. A few days later Poland was to bend to the will of the Nazi invaders. Only Warsaw, the capital city, held out for a month longer. Once more, I was at the mercy of the Nazi terror. I had run away from it in Peine, and it had caught up with me in Lodz.

As the first *Wehrmacht* troops marched into Lodz, they were joyously greeted by thousands of ethnic Germans pelting them with flowers and shouting, "*Sieg Heil!*"

But for the three hundred thousand Jews living in the city, darkness covered the earth. Classes at the Jewish high school ceased. Our days turned into a nightmare, and you could no longer feel you were in charge of your own life. We were overwhelmed by a dreadful premonition. Everywhere antisemitism came out of hiding and erupted into the open.

One day, as I was passing the Jewish high school, I saw soldiers dragging some Jews into the entryway of a building. They kicked them, screaming vile abuse; they beat them and cut off their beards and side curls. Shocked at what I had seen, I ran home. I felt as though I were suffocating, I couldn't breathe, all my muscles tensed. On the way, I had to hide several times to escape similar attacks by other soldiers. These brutal people had robbed us of our human rights; we became fair game for every psychopath in uniform.

A few months later we heard the first rumors that the Nazis intended to round up all the Jews and send them to a closed-off zone, a ghetto.

My family had an intense discussion about what we should do, and it was decided that my older brother Isaac, who was twenty-nine, and I, fourteen, would not go into the ghetto. Instead, we were going to try to make our way several hundred miles farther east. The idea was to cross the Bug River at the new Soviet-Polish border and join up with the Russians. We thought we would be out of danger there.

My other brother, David, who was in the Polish army, had been taken prisoner by the Germans. My sister, Bertha, was going to stay with our parents for the time being.

Isaac and I hesitated. We didn't want to leave our parents; we wanted to help them and stand by them in these difficult times. But their decision, once made, was irrevocable, and they insisted that we get going. They were already old, they emphasized, and would share the fate of the other Jews in the city. We, on the other hand, were young and dutybound to use every opportunity to save ourselves.

"Didn't we bring you into this world to live?" my mother asked. Papa placed his hands on our heads and blessed us with the holiest Jewish blessing, that of the *Kohanim*, or priests: " ... may the Lord keep you ... and grant you peace." And Mama added, "You *must* stay alive!"

We left the house carrying backpacks we had stuffed with food for the journey, including an incredible amount of home-baked *Kommissbrot*, a type of bread my mother had prepared from special dough with cinnamon added to keep it fresh for months. My father looked disapprovingly at the load we were carrying; he thought it would only weigh us down unnecessarily. I was wearing the new suit I had worn at my Bar Mitzvah. We also wore, under some extra jackets and coats, several folding umbrellas buckled around us like belts. These umbrellas were then a brand-new invention and therefore quite valuable. We expected they would come in handy because we could exchange them for food or use them to pay Polish peasants for taking us along in their horse-drawn carts. My brother, who had worked for a firm in Lodz called Gentleman, had been able to salvage a few of these umbrellas at the last moment, just before the firm was looted.

In spite of the many dangers all around us, we managed to get to Warsaw by train. There, we were taken in by Mr. Silberstrom, the director of the Polish head office of Gentleman, which manufactured and sold raincoats, rubber boots, and those collapsible umbrellas. Because of his business dealings with the firm, my brother knew the Silberstroms well. He had often stayed with them while he was on his business trips. We spent four days with them, gathering as much information as possible so that we could better assess the situation.

Dozens of different opinions and contradictory rumors were circulating, making us uneasy and hesitant about what to do next. We had to decide which way to go and could only pray that it would be the right course. . . . Was it still possible to get on a train? Were they still running? Were the Russians keeping people from crossing at certain border points? And what about the muggers and thieves who terrorized travelers everywhere?

In the end we took a train going in the direction of the Bug River. It was jammed. Since I was rather skinny and short, I had relatively little trouble getting a seat, but my much bigger brother almost didn't make it onto the train. The compartment was oppressively cramped, and the air was stifling. The train moved awfully slowly, a seemingly endless trip. But at last we stopped in a small town about sixty miles from the river. About twenty of us got off the train there, all the others much older than I. We would have to walk the rest of the way. It was bitterly cold and windy; the snow was piled in drifts as high as the straw roofs of the nearby houses.

In exchange for a few coins, some Polish peasants agreed to take our baggage on their horse-drawn cart. Enveloped in the steamy clouds formed by the horse's breath, we trotted along behind the cart that was carrying our things, like a mourners' cortege following a hearse. Our tedious plodding through the crunching snow made me think of the expulsion of the Jews during the Spanish Inquisition, and I imagined that I was hearing the melody of Ravel's *Bolero*, endlessly repeated, during this long trek.

Now and then the peasants stopped to point out a nearby German army post. Then we would resume our silent march. Whenever I sensed Isaac's worried sidelong glance, gauging the regularity of my steps and checking to see how I was holding up, I would walk very erect and smile back at him reassuringly.

We reached the shore of the river the third week of December 1939, exhausted but alive. Red Army soldiers wearing green caps were clearly visible on the opposite bank.

Many other groups of refugees had also arrived at this spot, and all were looking eastward. A single small boat that belonged to a Polish peasant served as a ferry. The refugees began to mob the boat; they pushed one another, some even coming to blows; everybody wanted to be among the first to get on. Somehow I made it, but my brother was shoved back on shore. The overloaded boat cast off. Several people jumped into the water trying to catch up with us, hoping to get across the river by holding on to the side of the boat. I screamed my brother's name, yelling with all my might, but I couldn't see him anymore. Finally in all the tumult I heard him shouting to me, "Wait for me on the other side."

The peasant rowed quickly with powerful strokes. Ice floes rammed into the boat; the strong current threatened to pull us downstream. We had already crossed the middle of the river when the expression on the boatman's face turned to one of fear and horror. He sputtered, "Holy Jesus and Mary!" and crossed himself. I saw that water was seeping into the overloaded boat, and slowly but surely it was sinking into the icy waters. We weren't that far from the opposite bank, but panic broke out. Some of the refugees tried to save themselves by swimming to shore. Catastrophe was not long in coming: the boat with all its passengers capsized. Most of the grown-ups could stand on the river bottom and were able to wade ashore balancing their packs on their heads. But I was not tall enough; my feet found no hold. I started to swallow water while trying to hang on to passing ice floes. Encumbered by the many layers of clothing I was wearing and the collapsible umbrellas strapped around my waist, I couldn't even swim. None of the boat people came to my aid. But luckily a Russian sentry saw that I was in danger of drowning; without a moment's hesitation he jumped into the water. After he had pulled me up on the bank and I had caught my breath somewhat, I gave him the fountain pen I had received as a Bar Mitzvah present.

The next day my brother arrived, and we continued on our way eastward, toward Bialystok. The Nazi danger was now far behind us.

In Bialystok the streets and government offices were overflowing with refugees from western Poland. In accordance with the German-Soviet nonaggression pact, the western part of the country had remained in the hands of the German invaders, whereas the Red Army occupied eastern Poland. The Bug River flowed between the two armies like a dividing line.

Shortly after we arrived in Bialystok, a Jewish assistance organization for refugees sent me to a Soviet orphanage in Grodno, supposedly a safe place for me to stay. My brother continued northward to Vilna, where he intended to look up his old girlfriend Mira Rabinowitz.

The orphanage (Dietski Dom, No. 1) was at 15 Orzeszkova Street in a magnificent manor house that belonged to a Polish aristocrat—at least that's what we were told. This wealthy property owner had fled when the Russians entered the city and had sought refuge with the Nazis. What a crazy world! People were leaving house and home, some going to the east to escape the Nazis, others to the west to join them.

In the orphanage I could once again live like a normal human being, something I hadn't been able to do for quite some time. The nightmarish journey had profoundly disturbed me, and my mind and emotions were in a whirl. Gradually I calmed down and became my old self. Thanks to sympathetic teachers, I once more became used to a regular schedule. I ate good meals, slept in a real bed, learned Russian, attended classes, and sang in a chorus. It looked as though the orphanage offered everything to make my life happy. But I was homesick and tormented by uncertainty about what had happened to my family. Here I was, living securely, eating hot porridge or studying Bolshevik theory in *Kratki Kurs WKPB*, an ideological textbook written by Stalin—and I had no idea how they were getting along.

The worry gnawed at me and preyed on my mind, and the physical symptoms associated with my mental anguish were not long in coming. I started wetting my bed. Every morning, while my classmates made fun of me, I had to take my sheets outside, air them out, and let them dry. This had never happened to me before.

We spent our days studying the usual school subjects and engaging in artistic pursuits. Every evening, clean and neatly dressed, we entered the large dining room of the orphanage for a communal supper. We usually had farina soup, which I liked very much because it reminded me of a dish my mother used to make quite often. After the meal the room was used for musical performances.

One day, as I was enjoying the delicious thick soup, one of the teachers came over and asked me to go to an adjoining room where someone was waiting to see me. Who could it be? Maybe a student from the neighboring orphanage who wanted to ask me about some homework. Or someone from the drama class. I even thought it might be Mrs. Kobrynski, with whom I had stayed a short while before entering the orphanage. Perhaps she had news from home. I left the steaming soup and hurried next door. No sooner had I shut the door behind me, when a weeping young woman threw her arms around me. It was my sister, Bertha! At last a ray of sunshine had pierced my loneliness. We kissed and embraced for a long time. I wanted to say something, but the words were drowned in a flood of tears; I was in complete turmoil. Bertha wouldn't let go of me. I could only stammer disjointedly trying to express my enormous happiness.

Staring at Bertha, I couldn't believe my eyes. How beautiful she was! I still remember her that way today. And yet I also saw in her face traces of the terrible suffering that separation from our family and the subsequent flight had caused. She was carrying a miserable-looking bundle and looked exhausted. She was only twenty-one years old, but life's trials already had left deep marks on her face. An hour later, after we had calmed down somewhat from the first wild joy of our reunion, we sat down on my bed, the only corner of privacy available, and talked. She didn't want anything to eat, she said, because she didn't want to leave me, not even for a second. The story of her adventures was alarming. She and a girlfriend had been able to escape through the gates of the ghetto, which were closed permanently only a short while later. She had followed the same route to the Bug River I had taken, experiencing similar dangers and complications. She found me by going to the return address I had put on the letters I mailed to my family in the ghetto.

Things were going reasonably well with our mother and father, she told me. They were glad to hear that Isaac and I were in a safe place, and they had decided to send her to the east too. There was nothing worrisome in the letters my brother David was writing from the German prison camp where he was being held.

Bertha slept a few hours in one of the unused beds, and at dawn the next day we parted again. She went to Smorgon, near Vilna, where she planned to stay with Isaac and Mira, who had just been married.

I couldn't know that this was to be the last time I would see her. Today, as I write these lines, her photograph stands on my night table like an ever-fresh flower.

In spite of my fears, I studied hard. About once a month I was overjoyed to receive a postcard from my parents. That's how I found out that they were well, that David had been released from prison and had come to the ghetto. There, he married his sweetheart, Pola Rosner. I answered their cards with long letters written with a shaking hand, addressing them to Family Perel, 18 Franziskanska Street, Ghetto Litzmannstadt (the name the Germans used for Lodz).

In the meantime, I had been accepted into Komsomol, the Communist youth group. I couldn't possibly know then that in the near future I would belong to quite a different youth organization.

It hadn't been easy for me to advance to the Komsomol from the Pioneers, the group to which the youngest boys in the orphanage belonged. The reason was that on my application form I had innocently and trustingly said my father was a businessman—a naive admission that I did not come from a proletarian background.

Indeed, this question was seriously discussed in the secretariat of our Komsomol. But because I showed such "outstanding progress at school and diligence in all subjects" they agreed on a compromise: even though I was of petit bourgeois origins, I was granted one month of probationary membership in Komsomol.

At the end of the month I was able to convince the admissions committee that I was a suitable candidate for membership. Finally I was accepted by the organization to which I had wanted so much to belong. The day on which party membership cards were ceremonially handed out was a very special red-letter day for me.

A bit of background may be in order here: In Peine we had lived at 1 Am Damm. In the house to our left, at number 6, was Mr. Kratz's grocery store. He was also the secretary of the KPD Ortsgruppe Peine, the local branch of the German Communist party. Almost every morning Mama would send me to the store to get fresh rolls and milk, and he always affectionately patted my head. Once he gave me a hammer and sickle badge to pin on my chest. I liked that a lot. And, of course, all my childish sympathy went out to his Red comrades when the brown-shirted SA gangs arrived in trucks to break up their meetings in the Luisenhof. The street fights that followed were bloody, and my prayers were always with the Peine Communists. It seemed odd to me then, but when the police finally did arrive, they invariably arrested those who had been attacked, not the brown-shirted vandals.

Then, after we left Peine and came to Lodz, my first friends there, Jacob and Jerzyk, were from families who belonged to the extreme left socialist Jewish *Bund* party. And so fate would have it that I continued to be exposed to the same views as those expounded by Comrade Kratz in Peine. I attended the Communist cultural club quite regularly and even took an active part in the outlawed May Day demonstrations. Politically, at least, things weren't going to be any different for me in the Soviet orphanage in Grodno. The white shirt with the red Pioneer tie and the daily lessons in Marxism/Leninism fell on fertile soil: Solly Perel became a devoted participant in the class struggle for a better future for mankind!

For cultural and artistic purposes our orphanage was linked to a Red Army armored regiment, and we routinely spent evenings in the company of officers and soldiers from this unit. They taught us wonderful songs like "Kalinka" and "Katjusha." Years later I sang these songs in Hebrew with my buddies in the *Palmach*, the striking arm of the Haganah, during the Israeli war of independence.

During these get-togethers, friendly ties were established between the children of the orphanage and the soldiers. They sometimes invited us to come to their barracks and watch or even participate in various sporting events. All these things helped to cheer me up.

Now and then the soldiers took us to the local movie theater, where Russian films were shown. One day we saw *The Search for Happiness*, a film about the Jews of Birobidzhan. I didn't understand any of it. Who were these Jews and how did they get to eastern Siberia? But in some of the scenes they were speaking Yiddish, and that made me happy. I resolved to visit the place called the Jewish Republic. However, impending events kept me from doing anything about this far-fetched scheme.

Two years passed—1939 to 1941. Then, in June, we were busy with last-minute preparations for our departure for summer camp in the unspoiled open country along the shores of the river Neman. Having spent the previous summer in the same area, we were all waiting impatiently for this wonderful time to begin.

We had no inkling that at this very moment the German army was preparing to attack. The countdown had begun for Operation Barbarossa, Hitler's invasion of the Soviet Union.

June 22, 1941. The attack began before dawn. At 5 A.M. the din of the first German bombs startled us out of bed. A few minutes later we found out what was happening: the Germans had broken the German-Soviet nonaggression pact and had begun their invasion of Russia. One of our Soviet teachers, a Jew, suddenly appeared in our dormitory and ordered all Jewish children to get dressed. We were to flee into the interior. Meanwhile, loudspeakers had been set up everywhere, and you could hear the voice of Soviet Foreign Minister Vyacheslav Molotov reading a declaration of war "to defend the sacred motherland."

A large group of us took to the road. We thought the Red Army would make short shrift of the fascist invaders, would decimate them with their roaring, whirring war machines even before we made it to Minsk. Anyway, that was what the patriotic Russian songs we sang said, and that was the gist of what the Communist party bigwigs were saying in their speeches, which never stopped promising the annihilation of any enemy who dared to set foot on Soviet soil.

But an entirely different picture soon emerged: what we were seeing was the defeat of the "glorious, invincible Soviet army." The roads and fields were strewn with dead and wounded. Fires burned everywhere; the air was thick with acrid smoke. The stench of decaying corpses assailed our nostrils. The people in my group panicked, everyone running off in different directions.

Now I was alone. I wanted to keep going north, toward Smorgon, to reach my brother Isaac. But a wave of refugees carried me eastward to a small village near Minsk. There I found out that fleeing farther east was no longer possible; the Germans already had captured the city of Minsk. There was horrible destruction and devastation everywhere.

It was hard to keep a clear head during this nightmare. Only two days before, like thousands of others, I had fled. I had jumped off an overturning horse-drawn cart, had clung to a truck filled to capacity, with only one thought in mind: to stay alive.

The earth began to burn under a hail of bombs and grenades. Thick columns of smoke rose to the dark sky. The whistling of the death-dealing explosive shells was getting louder and coming ever closer. To escape the shock waves from these explosions, I had to throw myself to the ground and crawl to a sheltering rock or huddle under a tree root. Above our heads we heard the endless drone of the Nazi planes.

No wonder this invasion was called a *Blitzkrieg*, a lightning war. It was characterized by powerful columns of tanks advancing into the interior of enemy territory without concern for what was happening on their flanks. Once they reached a certain point, the tanks swarmed to the right and left. Then, branching out, they would meet up with the other armored columns operating parallel to them. In this way, within a few days, the Germans succeeded in driving spearheads from the north to the south and along the entire front line that they controlled. The Red Army was encircled by these spearheads as if by pincers.

The situation was becoming critical—fires, the wounded, and the dead were everywhere. . . .

I was sixteen years old.

But I think it was my youth that allowed me to stay relatively calm and to keep my wits about me. Of course, I couldn't have known what real danger I was in. Nor could I picture what the future held. For a time I had been successful in escaping the hell of the Third Reich. I had escaped from Peine, Lodz, and now Grodno. My present flight from Grodno to Minsk seemed to be almost over. Actually, it had only begun.

Early in the morning on the day after I arrived in the little village, I came upon some senior Soviet officers bent over a map they had spread out before them. Junior officers were rounding up scattered soldiers, trying to form them into an orderly unit, in the hope that they could then break through the German encirclement and meet up with the regular units. I never found out whether they managed to do it.

I had discovered some noodles and sugar in a field mess that the Russians had left behind during the headlong retreat, and I was on my way to the nearest well, where I wanted to fill a pot with water in which to boil what was left of the noodles and the last pieces of sugar.

The shell bursts were coming closer. Pilots in low-flying planes were firing machine-gun salvos, and random bullets whistled through the air. Once again the earth itself offered me the only available protection; I was able to find a degree of safety behind a hill, a rock, a rise in the ground, or a roadside ditch.

And then, they suddenly appeared.

After the clouds of dust had blown away, I recognized them clearly. Their faces were blackened with soot and encrusted with dirt. Large driver's goggles covered their foreheads and their eyes. Ready-to-fire machine guns were mounted on the sidecars of their motorcycles. The fear-inspiring steel helmets, the verdigris-colored uniforms, and the black boots made them look like monsters.

Escape was impossible. We were trapped.

A low-flying plane swooped down, dropping leaflets that ordered us, in Russian and in German, to put down our weapons and to obey the commands of the men in the patrol vehicle that materialized before us.

Orders were shouted: *"Dawai! Dawai!"* *"Los! Los!"* [Come on! Come on!] We formed long lines in an empty field where a selection process was about to begin. I decided to stand in the longest line, made up of officers, soldiers, and civilians. I was the only child there. In spite of my sixteen years, I looked like a little boy.

I waited in that line for hours as it slowly moved forward toward the German guards. One rumor after another made the rounds. There were whispers that the *Wehrmacht* wasn't going to put Jews and Red Army political commissars into prison camps, as prescribed by the conventions of war, but was going to herd them into a nearby forest and shoot them.

Soldiers from the German commando unit guarded us carefully. Any careless step out of the line drew curses, threats, and gunshots. I saw Russian officers near me removing the badges from their uniforms; others surreptitiously took off the five-pointed stars they had worn on their sleeves. These were the insignias of the *Politruk*, the civilians assigned by the Communists to assist the military officers.

Each step forward in the line was a step closer to death. Paralyzed by fear and dread, I couldn't think any more; my tongue felt like a lump of lead. I could barely murmur, "Mama, Papa, God, where are you? I don't want to die— not yet."

As if in a daze, without really having thought about it, with a courage born of despair, I managed to dispose of all documents that testified to my Jewish origins and my membership in the Komsomol. With the heel of my shoe I dug a little hole in the soft soil, shoved the telltale papers into it, and tamped the earth back down. All this under the guard's nose! I hadn't thought of the consequences or how these fanatics for order and perfection would react when confronted by a boy without identity papers. But there was something like an intuitive faith, a spark of hope, and an inner voice whispering, "Everything's going to be all right, nothing will happen to you. . . ."

A similar glint of hope probably flickers in the heart of anyone sentenced to death when the executioner opens his cell door and he must walk the last mile.

Ever since the end of the war, and even today, I dream I am standing at the edge of a freshly dug pit. Across the way, executions are being carried out . . . the bullets whistle . . . they hit or they miss. . . . I fall . . . fall . . . and awake in my bed. I am bathed in sweat, rigid with terror, I fight for breath, but I'm alive, I'm well. Each time I wake from that nightmare, it's as though the gift of life were given to me anew.

The line moved up. Soon the German soldiers were only a few feet away, with but a handful of prisoners between them and me. I could clearly see the faces of those who were deciding who would be permitted to live and who would not.

I heard them bark commands. Was my last hour about to strike?

At that instant I wanted to bolt, to vanish from the face of the earth, to turn into something else, some sort of animal perhaps, or to become invisible. How I wished I could wake up and find myself in my mother's arms! But nothing like that happened. I stood there, rooted to the spot. My fear had reached an indescribable crisis point. It spread through every fiber of my body and threatened to sunder it into thousands of pieces. Amid this unbearable tension I felt the release of a few drops of semen. The tension eased and a strange sense of relief came over me.

As though freed and suspended between heaven and earth, I closed my eyes briefly. When I opened them again, I saw the words *"Gott mit uns"* [God is with us] engraved on the belt buckle of a soldier standing to my left. What did these words mean?

Was this the same God who had designated the Jews as the children of the chosen people? Or did the Germans have another god who had to be pacified with human sacrifices? The man wearing the belt yelled, "Raise your hands over your head!" It was my turn. For a few seconds, maybe the last ones of my life, I thought about my father and mother, about all the beautiful and good things on earth, about my enormous will to live.

I was shaking all over. I raised my trembling arms, and the steel-helmeted armed guard came over to search me. Although I already saw myself dying, I did not break out in sobs. I stood there stiff as a poker.

He raised his hand, and the moment it touched my body, that powerful will to live surged through me with the force of a hurricane. Something fantastic was happening within me; an angel of liberation was suddenly watching over me. The paralyzing fear vanished. My leaden tongue was freed, and a feeling of confidence and courage flowed through me.

Almost casually I told the man who was soon going to decide my fate, "I don't have any weapons," and gave him a big smile.

He bent down and quickly frisked my pants. Glancing up, he asked menacingly, "Are you a Jew?"

Without hesitation I answered him in a firm, normal voice, "I'm not a Jew; I'm an ethnic German [*Volks-deutscher*]."

My life hung by a thread. I was in the hands of a soldier who had been poisoned by the madness of war and the lust for blood. In his eyes a human life wasn't even worth a bullet. And it was his will and his decision that would determine my future. Would he believe me?

Unexpectedly the danger became even greater and my situation turned almost hopeless: A young Pole standing behind me in line suddenly came forward and said to the German guard, pointing at me, "He . . . Jew!" I denied it desperately, half dead with fear. And then the most astonishing and incredible thing happened—I still can't quite grasp it. The Nazi soldier believed me; me of all people! The nonplussed informer got a resounding slap in the face for his outrageous behavior and was ordered to "Shut up."

I looked again at the soldier's belt buckle. For the second time I read "God is with us." What was going on in this man's heart at that decisive moment? Did some divine voice whisper to him, "This boy must live"? If so, then why me of all people? Would I ever find out, or understand any of this? Before my turn in line had come, many Jews had already gone through the checkpoint. They also wanted to conceal their origins. Since they didn't have a good command of German, they couldn't very well pass as Germans, and so they declared themselves to be Poles, Ukrainians, Lithuanians, and so on. But whenever the suspicious soldiers had the slightest doubt about a man, they ordered him to drop his trousers. If he was circumcised, they cursed at him and made him join the group headed for the forest. There he was shot.

Somehow the soldier had believed me.

With surprising courtesy he asked me to step aside. Meanwhile the selection process continued. While I was waiting, I heard the metal clang of the shovels digging graves for my Jewish brothers and I heard the machine-gun salvos close by. The marksmen were part of the *Einsatzkommandos*, members of a task force who followed on the heels of the advancing *Wehrmacht* units, not to participate in the fighting but rather to murder countless Jews and *Politruks*.

I continued to stand there, shaken by the unbelievable scenes taking place before my eyes. Those who were ordered to go to the right were taken into the forest of death; those ordered to the left were forced into a huge camp that had been set up for them. I stood in the middle awaiting my fate.

Now and then the German soldier who had just saved my life smiled encouragingly to show that he hadn't forgotten me. When a sergeant approached, the soldier said, "Sir, we found a young German among this human garbage." The sergeant smiled benevolently at me.

One of the major goals of the Nazis was to bring all ethnic Germans back into the Reich. The soldiers around me were therefore filled with patriotic pride at the thought that they were participating, in a small way, in the realization of such a great undertaking. They still had a long way to go until the thousands of ethnic Germans who lived on the shores of the Volga could be liberated, but with me they had at least made a start. About an hour later, a half-track full of soldiers and weapons drove by. The sergeant stopped them, exchanged a few words with a captain, and told me to climb up onto the hood of the vehicle. Those inside the half-track smiled at me. One soldier took a photograph of me, without knowing what a unique picture he had snapped. Not until 1987, forty-five years later, did I get a chance to see that

Sitting on the hood of a German half-track of the 12th Panzer Division, June 22, 1941, near Minsk, shortly after I had passed myself off as an ethnic German. My clothes and cap were the standard dress of my orphanage in Grodno. The living nightmare I was going through is clearly visible in my face. (Courtesy of Ehrenfried Weidemann.)

photo. I found it in Lübeck in the home of Ehrenfried Weidemann, the soldier who had taken me prisoner.

The half-track continued on its way after I had squeezed inside. The screeching of its treads drowned out the gunshots in the forest, and the clouds of dust it raised hid from view the countless people who were moving slowly toward their fate. . . .

My journey into an uncertain future had begun.

2

WITH THE *WEHRMACHT*

Inside the half-track I had to hold on with both hands; falling off would have been fatal. Fortunately, the drive didn't take long, and we soon arrived at the camp of the *Panzerjägerabteilung*, a battalion-sized anti-tank formation of the 12th Panzer Division.

The company first sergeant, a forty-year-old Berliner named Haas, welcomed me warmly. He said a few sympathetic words about my weak, confused condition and the nightmare I must have lived through, and promised to take care of me. I was famished. My clothes were not much more than rags, for in my headlong flight I often had to crawl through bushes and over rocky terrain.

A young soldier was told to bring me something to eat. I'll never forget the ravenous hunger with which I devoured an entire plate of sandwiches. Another soldier was ordered to fetch the gear I needed, along with boots and the smallest uniform he could find.

After I had eaten and washed up, I slipped into the *Wehrmacht* uniform. Looking at myself in the rearview mirror of a parked vehicle was like getting a slap in the face. Up to now my feelings and thoughts had been completely dominated by this endless nightmare in which I had no active part, in which I played the role of an extra. Yet everything seemed to have been scripted and predestined, and my guardian angel had hovered over me, had protected me, and had told me what to do and what to say.

On my chest I saw an insignia with the Prussian eagle holding a swastika in its predatory claws. They had given me a cap with a black-white-and-red band, and that sobered me totally. All around little Solomon—me—a bloodthirsty war was going on, and here I was in a Nazi uniform! An icy shiver ran down my spine. The situation was more than I could handle; I didn't know how to behave. I was afraid, not only of those around me but of myself. I'm not sure whom I feared more. I, a Jewish child, had joined the horrendous enemy. I had to summon up all my strength not to lose my self-control and to keep the dangerous truth from coming to light.

Ever since I could remember, I had been fleeing from these people, my heart filled with mortal fear and terror. And now I was in their camp, wearing their uniform, and pretending to have made it to safety and to my homeland. In the mirror, I saw the uniform on my skinny body, the same uniform from which I had been fleeing—first in Peine, then Lodz, and finally the Grodno orphanage. Maybe it was only a bad dream from which I would soon awake. But when I opened my eyes, I saw that this was my new reality. At first I refused to believe what my eyes saw. The craziest fantasy could not have envisioned such a reversal. What I was feeling could have been felt only by a lamb thrown into the lion's den. It took several minutes before I could cope with the shock of this abrupt change.

Now I thought feverishly about what I would say and how I should behave when the Germans questioned me. I was still deep in thought when they asked me to report to the technical sergeant, who was sitting in a blue Volkswagen that served the company as a mobile office. On a board next to the steering wheel was a typewriter. The back seat was filled with shelves full of administrative files, an example of German efficiency.

I approached him. Grabbing a pencil, he said, "Your papers, please."

My tongue stuck to the roof of my mouth and I could hardly swallow; that gave me a few seconds to think. If I were to tell him the truth, namely, that I had buried my papers in the ground, death would be inevitable. I knew I had to invent a plausible story. I had never learned to lie credibly on the spur of the moment, but the Nazis and the circumstances taught me to do that as I let myself be carried along by fantasies inspired purely by my need to survive.

Within seconds the lie was out: "Sir, all my identity papers were destroyed by the massive German artillery bombardment in the encircled territory where I was staying," I answered with self-assurance, not betraying the least bit of doubt about the credibility of my answer. "Oh, you poor guy!" the German said and smiled sympathetically. Putting a blank sheet of paper into the typewriter, he asked, "What's your name?"

Automatically I gave him my real name, Perel. And then, instantly, an alarm went off in my head. Solomon, what have you done? You've just destroyed any chance for survival— Perel is a distinctly Jewish name.

Obviously I hadn't had enough practice in deceit; I hadn't quite grasped what it was all about, that from now on every minute of my life would depend on concealing the truth and on spontaneously inventing lies, my only weapons of defense, without which survival would be impossible.

Luckily, he hadn't heard me say "Perel" because of the noise made by the bombs being dropped by the Stukas (German dive-bombers) and the roaring motors of the biplanes overhead, and so he asked again, "What? What was that?"

I had been granted a second chance. I had to give him another name, but it couldn't be completely different from Perel—nothing like Stuttwaffer or Müller. So I replied, "My name is Perjell."

Evidently that was a good choice, because a soldier who was standing nearby backed me up. "Ah yes," he explained, "Perjell is a typical name among Germans living in Lithuania." Of course, I agreed with him immediately. Later if anyone were to ask where my family came from, I could always answer, "Lithuania." After all, a name expert had testified to that. . . .

The second question followed on the heels of the first, "Given name?" Naturally, I didn't say Solomon; I would have been crazy to do that. Despair inspired me and I gave the first name that came to mind: "Josef."

That's how my new identity was created, with dire circumstances dictating my every move. And so I became Josef Perjell, an ethnic German from Grodno. The only true item in my file was the date of my birth. I didn't have to lie about that. After all, there were no specifically Aryan birth dates.

From that day forward, I, Solomon Perel, a Jewish boy from Peine, had to live secretly under a false name.

German efficiency and precision functioned perfectly. I was immediately assigned to the 12th Panzer Division of the German *Wehrmacht* and its First Sergeant Haas and company commander, Captain von Münchow.

The news about me quickly made the rounds, and several men from the unit turned up to look me over and to welcome the new German boy "who had been part of the booty."

It's unbelievably difficult to smile and give the impression you're happy while inside you're torn by grief and fear. In spite of their politeness toward me, I feared the Germans like the plague. A single indiscretion could cost me my life.

I had to organize my thoughts and emotions, keep a cool head, and familiarize myself with a game whose rules I didn't know. At this point, I had no inkling that this was only the beginning of a crazy and never-ending comedy of horror.

I spent the night in the front seat of a truck. Despite the unbearable fear that held me in its grip, weariness at last won out, and I fell into a deep undisturbed sleep.

The next morning I was sent to the equipment room to pick up the essentials needed by a regular *Wehrmacht* soldier. Many different items had been meticulously placed in a big army duffel bag for me. I was busy washing up when I heard the order to line up. It was loud and repeated several times. I began to tremble and felt queasy. Fortunately, they exempted me from this particular lineup; I was permitted to stand on the sidelines. Roll call included a check of the soldiers' weapons and shoes, whether they had shaved, and their physical cleanliness, as well as the distribution of mail and the reading aloud of the order of the day. From what I heard, I gathered that the German military operation was going according to plan and the troops were moving rapidly toward their intended targets in the East.

Shortly after that, as I was lining up with other soldiers from the company, the technical sergeant came walking toward me holding a razor in his hand. I was so frightened, my stomach began to hurt. My face must have shown my confusion. Bending down, he smilingly apologized, saying he was about to remove the national emblem of the Reich from my uniform because I had not yet sworn the oath to the Führer and to the German people. Therefore I was not considered a regular soldier and could not wear the emblem. He consoled me with the promise that at the first opportunity I would be allowed to take the oath and the national emblem of the Reich would then be officially restored to me.

Day and night I thought of only one thing: escape. I wanted to reach the most forward sector of the front, cross the line, and join the Soviet army combat units. But I soon realized how impossible this was at the moment and decided to wait for a more favorable time.

Meanwhile, because I spoke Russian, they had given me a broad armband to wear. It said *Dolmetscher* [interpreter]. And before long they led me to a temporary prison camp that had been set up in the vicinity. I was supposed to act as interpreter during the interrogation of several captured Russian officers. Thousands of prisoners, guarded by armed German soldiers, were crowded into this huge camp. Their heads had been shaved, and they were sitting cross-legged in the searing sun without water or food.

As I entered the enclosure, I noticed a wounded man lying on the ground dressed only in a Russian military jacket. The lower half of his body was naked; there was a deep wound where his genitals should have been. He was groaning and pleading for water. I thought of the Russian soldier who had saved me from drowning. But I had neither the means nor the opportunity to help this man. I whispered a few consoling words in his ear and, with a heavy heart, followed the two German officers who were accompanying me.

The barracks housing the captured Russian officers were surrounded by a fence and tall trees. In contrast to the countless regular soldiers, the officers were given preferential treatment, and so they still looked like civilized human beings. I was ordered to translate the camp regulations, which included rules for maintaining order and the punishments for violators.

My duties as interpreter weren't particularly difficult, and I was amazed at how quickly I got the hang of it. Every time I encountered the Russian prisoners, with whom I felt a natural solidarity, I had to conceal my sadness over their defeat and humiliation. Gradually, my faultless behavior at the interrogations and investigations gained me the trust and respect of my German "comrades." They thought I looked funny in my too-big uniform and huge boots—like Puss-in-

Boots. I was called the "youngest soldier in the *Wehrmacht*," and that made them like me even more. They were constantly stuffing me with sweets, asking me how I was feeling, and seeing to it that I wasn't too hot during the day or too cold at night. They also started calling me *Kumpel* [buddy]. I became the mascot of the company and was the first with whom they shared the packages they received from their families.

These men, the enemies of my family and my people, who, had they known my secret, would have killed me, saw me as a talisman who would assure them of victory and keep them from bodily harm—while I was secretly praying for them to perish and lose the war. What bitter irony!

The battle cry, "Forward, to the East!" echoed with every step we took. We advanced several miles every day until we came within range of the outer city limits of Smolensk.

Generally speaking, strict discipline prevailed in our outfit. The men were especially afraid of First Sergeant Haas. Captain von Münchow was rarely seen. A truck loaded with bottles of wine and champagne followed us as we moved east. The captain spent a large part of his free time in this truck in the company of officers from nearby units. If by chance I found myself alone in his bunker, I would use the opportunity to swipe a cigarette from his desk, light up, and smoke it with relish.

Our outfit, moving forward independently of other units, consisted of several dozen vehicles led by the captain's car. From time to time, the duty officer or the technical sergeant would drive his motorcycle the length of the convoy to make sure that the men had all their equipment with them, were wearing their helmets, and were ready to use their weapons. The jackets of our battle uniforms had to be buttoned up to the top button. Only during the hot hours of the afternoon, when the sun beat down, did the captain deign to remember us. Then he gave the order, "Open the top button!" and the word was passed along from vehicle to vehicle. I sat in the back of the second car and was allowed to pass along the good news. Then, for some time, I watched what was happening down the line in the rest of the convoy. Just as in a slow-motion film, one head after another turned around to pass on the order, and one hand after another was raised to unbutton the topmost button.

The unit's medical officer, Heinz Kelzenberg, and I became friends. I would usually ride in his car in the convoy. We ate together, and whenever we were resting by the side of the road, he would tell me about his family, his hometown, Cologne, and Germany in general. He taught me to sing a few folksongs in the Cologne dialect, and I became very attached to him. He was tall, had a fine face and light blond, carefully combed hair that was parted in the middle. It was he who first gave me the nickname Jupp, which the others quickly adopted. Soon there wasn't anyone who called me Josef any more; I was Jupp, the little interpreter.

Our unit advanced rapidly, especially during the daylight hours. At dusk we would set up camp on some favorable terrain. Watches and reliefs would be assigned, and preparations for the night were made. Billeting in the houses of the locals was out of the question because of the poor hygienic conditions there. We preferred to make our beds with bales of straw we found in nearby barns.

One night while I was fast asleep on my bed of straw, I felt a hand stroking the lower part of my body. I opened my eyes wide and saw Heinz's familiar face next to mine. Startled by his touching me in this unusual way, I quickly moved aside, but he tried to get closer to me, whispering, "Be quiet, Jupp, I just want to play with you a little." I didn't understand what kind of game he wanted to play, but despite my natural naïveté I didn't want anything to do with this unfamiliar pastime. I picked up my blanket and went to sleep in another corner of the barn.

The next day we both behaved as we always had before, pretending that nothing had happened during the night. Obviously I couldn't afford to alienate one of the German soldiers. It would have been sheer madness to start a fight with anybody!

Some time after that, we set up quarters in a large school building. Communist slogans and color photographs of Stalin and his beloved daughter Svetlana still hung on the walls. A red tie fluttered gaily on her white blouse, and her broad smiling face radiated pride and happiness. She was giving the Pioneer salute: Always prepared!

I remembered how my father had once lifted me up and had circled round and round with me in his arms. I heard a surge of laughter from the past. Now I was a lost child surrounded by the devil's accomplices.

I stayed behind in one of the classrooms, and even though I was overcome with homesickness, I fell asleep. Suddenly I felt a damp rag on my face, and the sharp odor of ether stung my nostrils. Pushing the rag away with all my might before the ether could make me lose consciousness, I jumped to my feet, and there was Heinz standing in front of me, mumbling, "It really isn't that bad. . . ."

Of necessity, I had learned by now how to act in my new persona, had become used to it as though it were my second skin. Gradually the shock and homesickness abated and tormented me less frequently. My strong will to live eclipsed everything else, making it all seem less important.

We stayed near Smolensk for a few days. Here I had the opportunity to participate in a historic incident. I was called to the company's main camp as interpreter during the questioning of a senior Russian officer who had just been captured. Encounters like this always gave me secret pleasure, since my sympathies were all with the prisoners. It made me feel better to be able to befriend them surreptitiously or sneak some food to them. This was my pathetic contribution to our common cause, which consisted of holding out and surviving under such terrible conditions. My conscience had not yet been deformed by the new identity I'd been forced to assume, and my new personality was just beginning to develop.

A soldier on a motorcycle picked me up. After traveling for several miles we reached a little house with a straw roof; its owners had fled. This was where some of the Russian officers were being held. The faces of the junior officers and soldiers were marked by the horrors they had experienced prior to their capture. I sensed their fear and worries about what lay in store for them.

The guards pointed to one of the Russian officers, and the Germans, headed by First Lieutenant Henmann of the 2nd Company of the 12th Panzer Division's anti-tank battalion, approached him and immediately began the interrogation. I was surprised how formal and respectful they were. Usually they were arrogant and cruel to the Russians.

From the start of the questioning there was no doubt about the identity of this man. He was artillery officer Yakov Dzhugashvili, Stalin's son. While his famous father was hastily organizing the defense of Moscow, he was stuck here, a prisoner.

It was difficult to hide my excitement. Even the Germans lost some of their composure. After his papers were checked, confirming who he was, he was asked for details about the artillery positions of his unit, which was still engaged in battle. But he refused to give any information, and in accordance with his rights as an officer and prisoner of war, he merely stated his name and rank.

As soon as the division commander was informed, he ordered that the prisoner be immediately handed over to divisional headquarters. But there was still time for me to smile at him and wish him *"dobrovo puti"* [a good trip]. I never saw him again.

Hitler (in center of photograph) visits the staff of my *Wehrmacht* unit, summer 1941.

The *Blitzkrieg* continued and swept me along.

My way of life was completely changed by having to spend all my time among grown-up men. I had to listen to their vulgar talk, their lewd jokes, their stories about love and women, their boasts of sexual conquests. True, not everything they said was uninteresting, but mostly it was just shallow, vulgar gossip. Sometimes even they couldn't hide their longing for their families or their homesickness for Germany. But they consoled themselves by looking forward to the victory they would win long before the onset of the terrible Russian winter, a victory that would quickly bring them back home.

Not one of them ever dared to express a doubt or his own opinion about the war in which they were all involved, even though day after day the corpses of their fellow soldiers—bullet-riddled and torn by shrapnel—became more numerous. In the beginning the dead were still buried in individual graves, but the closer we got to Moscow, the more farm fields were turned into cemeteries.

As if brainwashed, the German soldiers incessantly repeated the same slogans. They felt reassured by the primitive conditions they found here. Just think, after twenty-five years of Communist rule, such slovenliness and weakness! Some paradise! One had to be grateful to Adolf Hitler for bringing them here to open their eyes to this kind of regime.

Here was the evidence that the Führer was right, that a guiding hand was needed in this benighted land, and that this hand designated by Providence could only be that of the German Reich. In the end the Ivans, as the Germans called their future vassals, would also benefit.

But sometimes life was fun. I was quite good on the harmonica and I learned to play their songs; they also taught me how to play Skat, a card game, and *Schunkeln*—swaying rhythmically to music with our arms linked—while the beer we guzzled ran down our hoarse throats. But even in the most boisterous moments, fear never left me. What if they found out—what would happen to me?

And so, always aware of my terrible secret, I lived a stressful double life. Wasn't there even one trustworthy soul among them in whom I could confide? I had a burning need to tell someone. But I learned to restrain my tongue, to watch my words, and to resist the dangerous temptation to share my secret.

One day Private Gerlach told me to report to the commanding officer of the company. He asked whether I knew how one approaches and salutes a superior officer. I assured him that I had been trying hard to learn these things and that I would not give him cause to be ashamed of me. I polished my shoes, beat the dust out of my uniform, and put my cap on straight. My heart was pounding, and I was torn by

contradictory feelings. I was afraid of Captain von Münchow, who always wore an extremely reserved expression
that dictated distance and caution. His uniform was be-
decked with ribbons, and the Iron Cross hung resplendent
on his chest. He was the son of conservative Prussian aristo-
crats, a Junker personified. To me he was the epitome of a
Nazi. Whenever I was anywhere near him, I tensed involun-
tarily. He had repeatedly expressed interest in me and inquired regularly how I was getting along. I always smiled and
said I was fine, but my smile scarcely masked the flush that
came to my face. Now I was afraid that he might become
suspicious and try to sound me out, or that he would make
inquiries and discover the truth behind my stammering answers to his questions.

I was supposed to report to his tent. Would this end up in
an interrogation for which I was no match and under which I
would break down? Silently I implored God for help.

Over time I had prepared a simple, convincing story that
was intended to dispel mistrust and spare me troublesome
questions. I would tell him that I had been orphaned at a
very young age (that's why I had been placed in the Grodno
orphanage); that I could scarcely remember my parents and
didn't know much about any close relatives. In short, I was
all alone in the world. To make this sound more believable, I
had invented an aunt who used to visit me now and then and
with whom I spoke German—but I had no idea where she
was now.

Totally on the alert, I stepped out briskly like a soldier
reporting to his commanding officer. There were guards
posted at the entrance to von Münchow's tent. I stepped forward, clicked my heels, and saluted smartly. Inside the tent
the captain probably could hear me, and he would be
pleased. He smiled when I walked in and asked me to sit
down. Private Gerlach served wine and cake. Suddenly I had
qualms of doubt. Was all this a dream, or was it real? "Have

you ever tasted wine?" the captain asked. I said no. I had learned my lesson. I was able to think the truth while, without blinking an eye, I was saying exactly the opposite.

Was the captain naive? I wondered. He should have realized that anyone at a Passover seder would have to drink at least four glasses of wine. I had liked these pleasant duties, or *mitzvoth*, that go with being a believing Jew. Once, before the traditional Shabbes meal, my father had dunked a piece of sweet challah, the braided Sabbath bread, in a strong alcoholic beverage and offered it to me to taste. I nearly choked, tears came to my eyes, and the people sitting around the table roared with laughter.

While I was thinking of these happy times in my father's house, I told the captain that the food in the orphanage was inedible and, of course, not a drop of wine had ever crossed my lips.

"If that's so, then here, try some really good wine—it's a German Moselle." The wine was pleasant, the cookies were delicious. What a nice war for the captain, I thought.

We relaxed into casual conversation. Surprisingly, Captain von Münchow showed not the least doubt or suspicion as I told him the fictional story of my life; it made him like me even more. He praised my courage, my perfect conduct, my excellent discipline. And then he made a stunning proposal.

He told me he owned a large farm, an estate in Stettin (now Szczecin) in Pomerania, was quite wealthy, but had no children. And since he liked me very much, he wanted to adopt me. . . . "Then you won't be an orphan any more, and you'll have a beautiful home in your new fatherland."

I was flabbergasted. Something inside me whispered, "How can you agree to that? You have your own parents! Wouldn't this be like committing a crime against them?"

My conscience rebelled, and I hesitated for several seconds. The most contradictory thoughts shot through my mind, and then I said, "I would like that very much." I even managed to look happy and to smile. He had no idea, couldn't possibly know, what was really going on inside me during those few seconds. On the outside I acted calm and seemed overjoyed, but within me a storm was raging. Pain, homesickness, tears threatened to overwhelm me. . . .

The adoption process was to be initiated right after the war was won, after the glorious return of the troops to the Reich. I would be reunited with my adoptive father on his estate. There the necessary formalities would be taken care of.

My "future father" chatted cordially with me a little while longer. As we said good-bye, he embraced me and said, "Your name will be Josef von Münchow. I will tell my wife that you agreed. She will be overjoyed and will surely write to you soon."

I stepped out into the fresh air, still in a daze and silently calling for my father and mother.

It seemed that the soldiers' excitement and eager expectation of an imminent and inevitable German victory had infected me too. Before I fell asleep at night, I would try desperately to picture the von Münchow estate and my adoptive mother, but I also thought of my own family. Would I ever see them again? I asked myself, "Will you ever be Solomon Perel again, or will you become Josef von Münchow for the rest of your life?" Even today I still marvel that all this didn't drive me mad.

And yet I never stopped thinking about how I could escape to the front line and join the Soviets. I knew that I belonged with the other side in this war and that my "desertion" would in some measure avenge the victims of the Nazis.

One day the opportunity arrived—or so I thought. I was ordered to go to a position that had just been taken by the Germans. In their headlong flight the Russians had left behind a radio transmitter that was still functioning, still receiving reports from the other side. I was to monitor these messages. The Germans were hoping to get information about Russian plans for an attack and thus accelerate their own rapid breakthrough. There was constant machine-gun fire in the area, but luckily the trenches led right up to the spot where the soldiers had found the transmitter.

I looked around me surreptitiously, sized up the distances, and planned my escape. An open, sloping field stretched out before me, at the far end of which, about two hundred yards away, there was a dense stand of birches.

The thought that only two hundred yards lay between me and freedom was very exciting. But I didn't know how to take the first step. I was surrounded by German soldiers who were constantly watching me, not because they suspected that I might want to escape, but because they wanted to make sure nothing would happen to me. They kept reminding me not to rely on my steel helmet for protection and never to stick my head out of the trench. All around us were freshly dug graves holding the still-warm corpses of German soldiers and marked by crosses made of birch branches nailed together. These carried the inscription "He died for his Führer, his People, and his Fatherland."

When we reached the transmitter, the soldiers asked me to put on some earphones and translate what I heard. I hesitated. Should I translate word for word, or should I distort the message so that it would have no informational value? Luckily, I couldn't understand anything because of the incessant racket of the battle going on around us. I did make out a few words, but they made no sense. Pretending eagerness and curiosity, I asked the radio operator to tune the transmitter so that the signal would come in more clearly, but his headshaking and curses made it plain that nothing could be done.

The soldiers decided to take me back to the base immediately. I begged them to let me stay there a while longer, using the pretext that this was my first time at the front and I wanted to follow the action. Actually my idea was to wait until after dark and then, at the first chance, to crawl to the birch forest. But they didn't give in and told me emphatically to come back with them. "Hostilities could start up again at any moment; then it'll be pure hell. Only an idiot would stay here if he didn't have to," one of them said with a smile.

It was really hard to get away from them. So I had to content myself with praying and hoping for a more favorable opportunity in the future.

Disappointed, I returned to my unit, where the men wanted to hear every little detail about the dangerous mission in which I had been the principal player. I made a big deal of it, and they liked that. Their opinion of me went up a notch.

One typical incident shows how highly they thought of me. I was having a minor argument with one of the unit's least popular soldiers, who never washed and always smelled bad. We were shouting at each other, and at one point he flew off the handle and accused me of behaving like a Jew. The others reacted instantly. They doused him with water, cursed him for his outrageous behavior, and demanded that he apologize to me. I was both astonished and confused. What was it he had to apologize for? Good God! If they had known that this dirty slob was right! Once again it was clear that my safety and my life hung by a slender thread.

That week the German soldiers fighting on the eastern front had their first bitter setback. The campaign had been long and arduous. They had expected an easy victory in this "nice war" and talked with pleasure about their lightning defeats of the Poles and the French. But things didn't turn out as expected. The *Wehrmacht* headquarters report that said the Soviet leadership in Moscow had resigned was false. Stalin was personally directing the defense of the city. Moreover, the concrete and steel fortifications erected around Moscow had held out. In addition, we were receiving confusing and contradictory information from within the city. And on top of all that bad luck, there were signs that the Russian winter was setting in. The soldiers had not forgotten Napoleon's defeat in 1812 and the poet's words:

Who could believe it?
Moscow burned to the ground,
Surrendered like that to the French!

They were scared out of their wits. And what made things worse was that the German high command and those responsible for a winter campaign had made no provisions for it.

Indeed, even though the advance of the German army units was slowed, they continued to push forward, crushing everything that stood in their way. I remember watching sadly as the half-tracks rolled through the golden fields of ripe wheat. And then, with delight, I saw the stalks trying to right themselves. Some succeeded, as if to say, "We, too, are not ready to bend before the conqueror; we won't make it easy for the occupying forces." And neither would I! This was one Jewish boy who wasn't going to knuckle under so easily.

In the meantime, we had taken up quarters in a large Russian village northwest of Smolensk. It was decided to give us three days of rest. Some "clever finaglers" in the unit had come up with a slaughtered pig, God knows how. They had also got hold of big kettles, pails, and washtubs for communal baths, personal grooming, and washing our clothes. We were sweaty and covered with dust. Several soldiers discovered a deserted peasant cottage and turned its large kitchen, which had a huge stove, into a bathroom.

Soon the water in the kettles was boiling and the kitchen quickly filled with clouds of steam and the singing of soldiers soaking in the tubs. They bathed together, in groups.

Of course, I couldn't participate in that. They would have seen that I was circumcised. I still remembered—and always would—the terrible selection scenes when the Germans first arrived.

On various pretenses I declined invitations to join this or that group in the bath, waiting patiently until the last man had left the kitchen.

Carrying a towel, a piece of soap, and clean underwear, I went in and carefully bolted the door. I stepped into one of the tubs; the hot water reached to my knees. Outside a soldier was playing a harmonica, and as I washed myself I happily sang along; it was an aria from *I Pagliacci*.

Suddenly I recoiled. Someone nearby was whispering something. Before I knew what was happening, a pair of strong arms grabbed me from behind. I felt a naked body pressing against me. I froze. Thousands of bells went off in my head. As the man's erect penis tried to enter me, I jumped as though a snake had bitten me. It would have been smarter just to stand there, with my back to him, but I had instinctively freed myself from his embrace. Jumping out of the tub, I turned around.

Heinz Kelzenberg, the medical officer, stood before me, a forced smile on his flushed, dark-red face. He seemed confused and disappointed that he had been frustrated. It was very quiet in the room. For some moments we stood there facing each other, naked as the day we were born.

What was bound to happen did happen. His eyes traveled down to my crotch. He hesitated, seemed baffled, and then asked, "Are you Jewish, Jupp?"

A deadly fear overwhelmed me. I murmured, "Mama, Papa, come, help me!" Breaking into tears, I pleaded, "Don't kill me! I'm still young, and I want to live."

Mental pictures of the horrors I had been forced to witness during the last several days rushed through my mind. In a small village, men from the German military police who had joined up with our unit had ordered the women to lock up all the village cats in a deserted house. And then the slaughter began. I'll never forget the sadistic joy they took in shooting at those poor animals through the half-open windows. The cats tried to avoid the whistling bullets, they cowered in the farthest corners, jumped high off the floor, meowing terribly, until finally there was a deathly stillness.

Now I stood naked and defenseless before a German officer, a toy in the grip of a gigantic annihilation machine, waiting for my death sentence. Perhaps it would be carried out with a shot from a revolver, just as in the case of the cats. And if he didn't shoot me on the spot, would he deliver me to the military police? For them it was routine to tear the clothes off men under suspicion and to hang a sign reading "I was a partisan" around their necks. On the women's chests they'd pin a sign "I'm a gun moll [*Flintenweib*]." After that, they strung them up on scaffolds set up in the marketplace or by the side of the road. That was intended to intimidate the local population, to keep them from joining the partisans who had begun to organize under the noses of the Germans.

As I write this, the thoughts I had during those moments that I was sure would be my last on earth come back to me. They were the thoughts one has before dying. . . .

Heinz came closer, gently put his arms around me, drew my head to his chest, and said softly, "Don't cry, Jupp, they mustn't hear you outside. I won't hurt you and I won't betray your secret. You know, there *is* another Germany."

Before he left the room, I had to promise him not to reveal my secret to anyone, especially not to my "future father," Captain von Münchow.

I dried my tears, finished my bath, and left the kitchen feeling much better. My troubling isolation had been lifted by a true friend. He had reached out to me as I was about to lose all faith in mankind, and to my surprise I discovered that not all those around me were potential murderers, not all German soldiers were convinced Nazis.

Later, Heinz and I sat under a tree, far from the others, and I explained the puzzle to him. I told him everything from the very beginning, about my family and our expulsion from Peine. I kept nothing from him of what had happened to me, and he listened sympathetically. I was sixteen; he was thirty and deeply moved by my loneliness. After that, he stopped making sexual advances, and a genuine and warm friendship formed between us. He promised to take me home with him after the war, and we swore to keep my dramatic story secret.

But several weeks later there was a terrible catastrophe. The rapid advance of the *Wehrmacht* forces came to a standstill near the Moscow suburbs. From then on, there was only back-and-forth trench warfare. It was the end of autumn.

The army high command decided that we had to be content with the surrender of Leningrad, which had been under siege for months, since at this time we couldn't take Moscow. So my division was redeployed northward in order to participate in the Leningrad operation. On the way, we heard a rumor that we, the front-line troops, would all get leave so that we could regain our strength. After the German victory in Russia, we would be transferred to France. The rumor was intentionally started to cheer us up. Now there ensued endless discussions about French wines, the famous French cuisine, and the fabulous, incomparable women. Each soldier imagined the most daredevil adventures. I'm sorry I didn't write down these unbelievable fantasies. But then, *I* also dreamed about France and its wonders, and would much rather have been there than at the front. I had no desire to stay here where I was in constant danger of being hit and killed by a grenade fragment or a stray bullet. Just think: to be killed by an ally's bullet while wearing the uniform of my

Бей жида - политрука,
рожа просит кирпича!

Комисары и политруки принуждають вас
к бессмысленному сопротивлению.

Гоните комисаров и переходите к немцам.
Переходите к немцам пользуясь либо лозунгом:

Бей жида-политрука,
рожа просит кирпича!

"Beat the Jew-commissar; his face just begs for a brick!" A German propaganda flyer encouraging Soviet troops to kill their political commissars and surrender, eastern front near Moscow, winter 1941. (Courtesy of Ehrenfried Weidmann.)

enemies! What a grotesque tragedy that would be. Yet, in the end, what difference does it make whose bullet kills you?

A short time later we reached the forests around Leningrad and began to prepare for the attack. They brought in "Goliaths" intended to break through the city's fortifications. These new and mysterious war machines were actually tiny patrol cars filled with dynamite. They were supposed to penetrate the enemy's fortified bunkers and then explode.

The Goliaths failed miserably, sinking into the mud of the deep swamps that surrounded Leningrad. Moreover, the Russians had invented a simple and effective machine called the Iron Ivan, a two-engine armored airplane that, without making much noise, was able to sweep low over the German convoys in the bright northern Leningrad nights, wreaking death and destruction. After they had dropped several bombs, which consistently hit their targets, the Iron Ivans would continue their precise attacks, with machine guns fired from the rear of the plane. We were ordered to jump from our vehicles and to shoot at them. But it was useless. These scenes were repeated almost every night: I remember the screams, the loading of the guns, and the shelling from the overhead planes. I would use as cover any object that seemed big enough, duck behind it, and watch this surrealistic spectacle. Yet despite all the setbacks and losses, the Germans let nothing deter them from fighting to take Leningrad. My unit set up quarters in the Schlüsselburg section; from there we could see the gleaming roofs of the city. Once again I was close to the front line. All around me military preparations were being stepped up. Heavy guns were emplaced in the rear, while tanks were brought forward and everyone dug himself a foxhole. The junior officers were ordered to the command post to get their instructions. H-hour had been fixed for dawn the next morning, and nervousness and tension increased among the soldiers. They all wanted to win quickly, to stay alive, and to make it through to the romantic leave they had been promised in France.

During the night the Iron Ivan had dropped leaflets signed by Marshal Kliment Voroshilov in which the Soviets declared they would defend the city to the last man. The enemy was no longer acting the way the Germans had expected. One hour before our attack was to begin, the Soviets opened fire. Our positions were subjected to massive shelling and mortar bombardment that cost lives and considerable matériel. In the midst of all this, I stood stock-still, as though in shock; it didn't occur to me to head for a safe place. Heinz saw the danger I was in. He threw himself on top of me and pulled me under a tank that was standing next to a tall building. The tank crew were already lying there in their soot-blackened uniforms. We nudged them aside to make room. The air was full of smoke and the acrid smell of burning.

A few minutes later Heinz was called away to care for the wounded. Before he left, he ordered me not to move from under the tank. I watched him as he ran off, bent over to make himself less of a target. There was a dreadful explosion and a blinding flash of light. I pressed my face into the ground and covered my head with my arms. Screams ripped the air. When I raised my head again, I saw Heinz lying on his back not far away, his face covered with blood. I crawled over to him and took him in my arms. Someone tried to close the deep wound in his neck, to pinch closed the artery from which the blood was gushing. In vain. His wide-open eyes stared into mine, and he murmured something I could not understand. Then he lost consciousness and died in my arms. To my dying day I will always remember him with high regard.

Heinz's death left me orphaned again, and I felt bitterly alone. I had lost my only ally and the hope and moral support I so desperately needed. A secret had bound us together; our relationship was one of absolute mutual trust. He took all that to the grave with him. "Once I had a buddy, there never was a better one . . ." (so begins an old German song: "*Ich hatt' einen Kameraden, einen bessern findst du nit . . .*").

Many of the soldiers in our unit were wounded, others were killed, and a lot of equipment was destroyed. Less than an hour after the attack had begun, the order "Get back in the trucks!" was issued.

Retreat. For the first time the proud conquerors were forced to turn back. Nobody cared any more about appearances, discipline, or whether the top button of your uniform was buttoned. They ran hither and thither, gathering the equipment that had been left lying around and loading it onto the trucks.

Then a headlong flight to get away from the bombardment started. On an impulse, I decided this was the time to escape. I was going to wait until the last German soldier was out of sight and then, with my arms raised, I would calmly give myself up to the advancing Russians. My heart pounded as I thought of the opportunity I now had. But again fate had something else in store. . . .

I hid in a latrine, hoping that in all the confusion my absence wouldn't be noticed. Through a knothole in the latrine wall I watched the chaos as the convoy of vehicles began to withdraw. I could see them preparing Captain von Münchow's command car for departure. Suddenly Private Gerlach yelled at me, "C'mon, Jupp, hurry! This is no time to take a shit!" I couldn't stay in hiding any longer; I couldn't escape—several of the soldiers were watching me. So I left the latrine, fumbling with my fly and belt as though I had just been to the toilet. Someone threw me a steel helmet, and once I was in the captain's car, he reproached me for being reckless, adding that, had I been a soldier, I would have been severely punished. But a crinkling around his eyes indicated that I shouldn't take his rebuke too seriously.

Leningrad was not captured. For their defense of the city, its citizens and soldiers deserve our unrestrained admiration.

Our unit was transferred to nearby Estonia. There, we were to recoup our strength, and our depleted ranks and equipment were to be replenished.

I was assigned as interpreter to Quartermaster Depot 722 Reval, which had its headquarters in the center of the capital, Reval (today Tallinn). We were entranced by the city's beautiful houses, palaces, and gardens. Unit 722 occupied a splendid municipal building. The men lived two to a room; the officers had been allotted spacious apartments. The job of the unit was to assemble and deliver supplies for the entire northern front. Trucks filled with goods arrived from many districts. With the help of Russian prisoners of war from a small prison camp nearby, these goods were reloaded onto freight trains going to the front.

Every morning there was a roll call in the prison camp to assign the work details. I had to translate the orders of the day into Russian, the type of work, the disciplinary rules, and punishments for negligence or theft.

The prisoners were an elite group, pleasant-looking educated men who were in good physical condition. Before long, a friendly and sympathetic relationship developed between them and me. More than once I would look the other way and smile when one of them hid a salami in his pants or made off with a big piece of smoked beef.

Once there was a minor incident involving one of the prisoners. Naturally, he and all the other Russians were just called Ivan by the Germans—just the way the Russians later, after the tables were turned, called all the Germans Fritz. We had met during a work break in a shack at the freight station. And there he made an odd remark: "I think it's interesting that you're the only one around here who doesn't roll his *r*s. You pronounce the *r* like a guttural *gh*. That's typical among Jews. For instance, you'd say *Abghasha* instead of *Abrasha.*" Without blinking an eye, I said that I didn't understand what he was leading up to and ordered him to get back to work with the other prisoners. After that, each of us went his own way, and the subject was never raised again. But obviously the man had guessed my origins. The thought that he might sow suspicion in other people's minds made me uneasy. But I had learned how to arm myself against the mortal danger that constantly hovered over me and how to handle it. I saw to it that, whenever I was with the Russians, there was never any doubt that I was a German soldier.

In Reval I met a charming young woman who was a few years older than I. Her name was Lee Moreste, and she lived at 3 Viruväliak Street. I went to see her practically every evening. One day her mother asked me, "Why are you Germans so cruel to the Jews?"

In that instant many thoughts flashed through my mind; above all, whether I should tell her the truth about myself. But I kept quiet and decided there and then to let her go on believing I was German. It could have turned into a dangerous situation; there was no way I could predict what her reaction would be. And so I told her I was not happy with what was going on, but that it was difficult to change things. I will always remember Mrs. Moreste for having asked this question. And I will never forget her daughter Lee, because she was the first woman in my life.

From time to time, Captain von Münchow would come to see me or ask about me. He was glad to hear that everything was all right, that I liked Reval and the work I was doing. But one day he brought news I didn't like: the army would have to let me go because I was a minor; I regretted this very much. My unit had been ordered to send me home to the Reich as soon as possible. A woman who had been delegated to accompany me to my new fatherland would be arriving shortly.

I had never wished, even for a second, to go back to Germany, which teemed with Gestapo and police. It would be like throwing myself into the lion's den because I knew that there I could neither hide nor escape in case of danger. So I scarcely heard the captain say how pleased he was that I was being returned to the fatherland. It was hard to produce a false smile and murmur a few words of gratitude.

Apparently he thought my confusion was merely due to this pleasant surprise. For the time being, he said, I was to return to my unit to wait there for the transfer order and the required discharge papers, and to say good-bye to everyone.

The Russian prisoners were sincerely sorry when they heard about my sudden departure. Before I left, Unit 722 presented me with several bottles of vintage liqueur and a superb French cognac. In Tartu, where my unit was resting and making preparations for the critical spring offensive, I received my military service record, signed by Lieutenant Colonel Becker, aide to the division commander. I was amazed when I read this report. After the Germans captured me, I had explained that all my papers were destroyed during the *German* artillery attack and I was therefore unable to give them proof of my identity. On the document they now handed me it plainly said, "We confirm that the ethnic German Josef Perjell lost all his identification documents as a result of a *Russian* artillery attack." This implied that I had given them my Aryan identification papers and only lost them afterwards. I'll probably never know, and I asked no questions about the motive that lay behind it. Was it just a mistake, or did Becker consciously want to help me? But, as a result, the authenticity of my papers could not be challenged. Furthermore, this new document also attested to Josef Perjell's exemplary conduct, keen judgment, and courage at the front. In addition, it asked that the responsible authorities help me to adapt to my new home.

It was obvious that this military certificate was worth more than anything else they could possibly have given me. And so I began to feel better about my new identity, thanks to this evidence of their regard, and the respect the document was bound to inspire in anyone to whom I would present it.

The military governor of the city of Reval now informed me that the woman who was to accompany me to my fatherland had arrived.

The die was cast. I had to leave these men to whom I had become so close. I must admit that because of the warm friendliness they showed me, I had learned to like them, but on another level I hated and feared them because they were *Wehrmacht* soldiers who committed crimes. In a final talk with Captain von Münchow I had to promise to write to his wife. He asked me to let him know soon where I was living and wished me a safe trip.

How had I managed for more than a year to survive in a unit of the German *Wehrmacht* that was famous for its extreme strictness, discipline, and harsh regulations? No one had tried to dig into my true origins or had even registered a single doubt; no one had asked about my original papers (after all, Grodno, my "hometown," was close by) or why I had joined the stream of refugees fleeing from the area after the German breakthrough. Why did no one ask me questions, suspect me, or start inquiries about me?

3

TO BRUNSWICK

In the office of the military governor, I met my escort, a functionary in the main office of the Hitler Youth in Berlin. She was about thirty-five years old, blond, attractive, and wore a good-looking beige-colored uniform. A swastika was emblazoned on her broad-brimmed hat, and there were several party decorations on her coat. I felt a pain in my belly. After reading my military conduct report, she expressed her admiration; the barriers between us came down and we were immediately on friendly terms. She explained the purpose of her mission, but in my confusion I understood only half of what she said. We decided to go shopping for civilian clothes and some personal items for me.

The next day we boarded a comfortable passenger train that was taking soldiers on leave from front-line duty back home. The light bulbs in the nearly empty train compartments had been painted over. It was very quiet, and you could tell the mood of the passengers was pretty dejected. We had a long ride ahead of us. From Estonia we were to go through all of Latvia and Lithuania and then through East Prussia to Berlin; it would take three days.

Up to that point I had been afraid of this trip into the land of a thousand dangers with its satanic regime, but I must admit that I felt strangely numb as I sat down in the train compartment. I would submit to my fate. I would rely on the all-powerful invisible hand that had so far governed my life, and I would entrust myself to it with faith and devotion.

I still remember the happy beaming face of the woman who was accompanying me, her pride in having been given the patriotic assignment of leading a lost child back to his German fatherland. How could she know that she was traveling with a young Jew, a son of Moses? I forced myself to talk to her as little as possible, so our polite conversation quickly turned into a monologue. She gave me an endless lecture about Germany's greatness, and while she held my hand tightly in hers, sometimes stroking me, she sang the praises of the German people and their Führer. She asked me to look at the cows grazing in the pastures we were passing and pointed out that they were covered with mud and dirt. In contrast, she said, German cows were clean and well cared for. The dirty cows led her to laud the cleanliness of the German people, to whom I also had the good fortune to belong. She added that we represented an elite, that our cause was just, and that we had been called to save humanity under the immortal leadership of Adolf Hitler.

This energetic woman didn't have much patience; she was in a hurry to turn me into a convinced National Socialist, even before we arrived in Germany. She talked incessantly. Only mealtimes and short naps stemmed the flood of her enthusiastic words.

During the second night of our journey something memorable happened. We were sitting alone in the dark compartment. The atmosphere was relaxed, and our conversation had taken a personal turn. I realized that she liked me, that she found my "beautiful pitch-black hair" particularly seductive. As a soldier at the front I had learned a few tricks, and so I paid her some compliments in return. Suddenly she stretched out on the bench and pulled me down close to her; mumbling unintelligibly, she covered me with passionate kisses. I was seventeen years old, and had a great deal of theoretical knowledge, thanks to the stories my army buddies had told. But up to that time the only woman I had gotten to know closely had been Lee Moreste. I couldn't resist the turmoil this woman on the train aroused in my young senses. These passionate embraces were sexual fulfillment for me, even if we didn't actually sleep together. Afterward I kept thinking, If she only knew . . . ! Even today I still regret that the circumstances prevented me from telling her the truth.

While I was living in Peine, we had heard a lot about *Rassenschande* [racial disgrace, having sexual relations with a non-Aryan]. A German woman could scarcely be guilty of a worse crime. Now I said to myself, "See, Miss Nazi, you've just been carrying on with a Jew!" I think she would have killed herself if she had found out.

We arrived in Berlin the next day. Until I received my permanent assignment, I stayed briefly in an elegant hotel and spent my time sightseeing. The hotel guests filled me with horror. They were elite officers, *Hauptsturmführer*, SS men wearing their death's-head uniforms, and SA chiefs in jodhpurs, brown shirts, black ties, and boots; but there were also Gestapo men in civilian clothes with cropped hair before whom all Jews and democrats trembled during those years. For the time being, they considered me a lost child, and I greeted them with *"Heil Hitler!"*

Whenever I climbed the hotel steps or stepped through a door, I would raise my arm in the Hitler salute. My escort was deeply moved by this; she had sewn a round conspicuous insignia—a swastika in a golden wreath of laurel leaves—on the lapel of my new suit.

I looked like one of them. Everyone had seen me calling out *"Heil Hitler!"* And I must admit that I was beginning to feel flattered and to enjoy the whole thing.

Today, some fifty years later, I realize that at the time a certain process had begun within me. The seed for my later identification with National Socialist ideology was planted during my stay in this hotel.

You have to try to imagine the mental plight in which I found myself. I was a lone fighter in a sea of swastikas, and my actions were intended only to delay the execution of the death sentence that had been pronounced on me because I was a Jew. I wanted to survive another hour, another month, perhaps a year; I simply wanted to stay alive.

I had to elude their smoothly functioning extermination machinery at any cost. But I didn't have a single weapon with which to defend myself, only their uniform and their insignias. And the fact that I am here now and can tell this story is because I learned how to behave like them and to play my Nazi role without hesitation. I relied wholly on my instinct of self-preservation, and it continually prompted me to behave appropriately. I gradually suppressed my true self. Sometimes I even "forgot" that I was a Jew.

Nothing kept me from enjoying the company of my escort and the beauty of Berlin's sights. I even went to the opera for the first time in my life. The German State Opera was performing Wagner's *Tannhäuser,* and for five hours I listened enthralled to this grandiose music. It was as if the stage sets and theatrical atmosphere had cast a magic spell over me.

However, when I was told where my future home would be—a boarding school in Brunswick—I felt like screaming, "Oh no! Not there!" Peine, where I was born, is near Brunswick, and someone there might recognize Solly, the Jewish boy from next door. It could be fatal. Germany was so big; it had many cities and boarding schools. Why did fate

have to pick this particular city? Why was destiny mercilessly mocking me?

Pushing these thoughts aside, I forced myself to smile
happily. When I recovered from the shock and was able to
think clearly once more, I told myself, "Since the course of
my life is following a peculiarly crooked path, it isn't leading
me straight ahead but is instead taking me back to the town
where my life began. I've come back to this place so close to
the town of my birth. I left there as Solly, and with the help
of a woman whose specific assignment it was to escort me, I
return as Josef. Is it really me who is coming back? I left as a
child; today I'm a young man with a different name. In spite
of that I am the same me. How can all this be true?"

*For many years there was one question I couldn't get out of my
mind: Why did they honor Josef Perjell by assigning this female of-
ficial just to me? I got the answer in 1987, in Heppenheim near
Frankfurt, at the first reunion I attended with my former army
buddies from the 12th Panzer Division. The invitation was sent to
"Josef Perjell, residing in Israel"—and Solly Perel showed up.
That's when they told me the following story: Captain Joachim von
Münchow's niece, Henriette, the daughter of Heinrich Hoffmann,
Hitler's personal photographer and art adviser, was married to
Reich Youth Leader Baldur von Schirach. (He was later sentenced
to twenty years in prison at the Nuremberg War Crimes Trials.)*

*Years later, this same Henriette von Schirach got in touch with
me when she heard about my story through the media. She sent me
a copy of her book,* Der Preis der Herrlichkeit,* *and said she
would very much like to meet me because she had something to give
me. But that meeting never took place. When I asked about her in
Munich in February 1992, I found out she had died earlier that
year. In any case, it was because she was von Münchow's niece that
the captain's request reached an official in the Reich Youth Leader-*

---

* Henriette von Schirach, *The Price of Glory*. London: Muller, 1960.

ship, who arranged to have me sent to Brunswick, accompanied by this special escort. Not until 1987 did I learn that I had been protected at such a high level. This doubtless explains the privileges I enjoyed.

But to get back to my story. After saying good-bye to my escort at a train station in Berlin and promising to write to her, I boarded a train to Hanover, where I had to change for Brunswick. The train went through several stations teeming with soldiers, all on leave from the front. Again and again I saw signs reading *"Räder rollen für den Sieg"* [Wheels must roll for victory].

During the entire trip I looked out the window of the train compartment, just to check if my escort had been right when she'd said German cows were cleaner. . . . Indeed they were, but what difference did that make? Did it justify the shameful, bestial behavior of the majority of her fellow Germans?

I was deep in thought when the train made another stop. Good God, I immediately knew where we were! As soon as I saw the sign PEINE, a remarkable feeling came over me. What strange turns one's destiny can take: This was where my painful journey eastward had begun, and now fate had brought me back to this place a second time. The memories associated with this train station belonged to my former identity, but they broke through the barrier separating the past and the present, and awakened an overpowering homesickness in me.

I stared at the station sign. Its white background was blackened with soot. The same brown smog that people used to complain about when I lived here still hung over the town. It came from the big iron and steel works, the Peine Rolling Mill. When the grade-crossing gates closed, traffic on both sides of town was brought to a standstill. Cars had stopped, bicyclists were waiting with one foot on the ground, and children laughed happily watching our locomotive belch smoke and steam into the air. I took in every detail, eager to absorb it all, and I couldn't help feeling that this was another world. The jolt of the train as it started up again put an end to this painful look at the forbidden place where I had spent my childhood.

A short while later we arrived in Brunswick and, following orders, I went to the office of the stationmaster. As I walked in, two young men in brown uniforms with the jagged lightning-flash insignia on their chests and swastika armbands on their sleeves jumped up from their chairs. Terrified, I thought, If I'm being met by people like this, where am I going to end up, into whose clutches will I fall?

With a trace of a smile one of them inquired whether I was Josef Perjell from Berlin. I nodded and he asked me to come with them. They were very polite, even helped carry my bags. We climbed into a brand new Volkswagen and drove off. My head was foggy, so I could only answer their friendly questions, which I didn't quite understand, with a short yes or no.

The streets were crowded with well-nourished people, and my initial impression, that I had arrived in a land of cannibals for whom I was about to become an easy and particularly tasty victim, began to fade. My mind was in a whirl, and at one point I almost asked, "Where are we going?" But my voice would have betrayed my fear, and so I remained silent.

After driving for about half an hour, we stopped in front of a large, modern building. Nazi flags were flying from its facade. I'll never forget the terror that swept through me.

The building seemed very well maintained. A huge inner courtyard served as a place for muster; a flagpole stood behind a stele and the bronze statue of a brave-looking soldier. The courtyard was bordered by two-story residential houses. There was an Olympic-size swimming pool, a cinder track, and various areas for gymnastics and team games. At the far

The main building, dormitory, and swimming pool at the Hitler Youth school, Brunswick.

end of the courtyard, on the gable of a tall neogothic structure, was the inscription *"Kraft durch Freude"* [Strength through Joy]. This building housed the dining room. Several blond youths were crossing the yard, all wearing black pants and brown shirts with Nazi insignias.

I realized that I had entered the lion's den. If—God forbid!—they had discovered I was Jewish, they would surely have torn me to pieces like beasts of prey. Once this terrible fear became lodged in me, I could never quite rid myself of it. Even today, I still feel its effects.

I was shown into the office of *Bannführer* [Major] Mordhorst. He stood up in all his splendor, surrounded by a royal entourage of subordinates, and greeted me with a brisk *"Heil Hitler!"* I had no choice but to pull myself together, raise my arm diagonally upward, and reply *"Sieg Heil!"*

Then we all sat down to talk and get to know each other. Facing me, behind the *Bannführer,* was a bust of Hitler, his eyes and mustache rendered particularly vividly. On the walls were photographs of Hitler Youths marching past the reviewing stand on the *Reichsparteitag* [Nazi Party Day] in Nuremberg. I was asked about the battles and the "glorious victories" I had witnessed. To this day I am amazed at how well I recounted these daring feats, without stuttering or hesitation. My listeners were impressed and fascinated. After I had been telling my story to this rapt audience for several minutes, the *Bannführer* proceeded to describe his organization for me. My worst fears were confirmed. I had landed in a Hitler Youth school, a National Socialist vocational training school, the only one of its kind in the entire Reich. This *Ritterburg* [castle] of National Socialist work had three principal goals: to train new generations of leaders for the various party organizations, to provide a political and technical education, and to do an effective job within the structure of Unit [*Bann*] 468.

The *Bannführer* explained that Hitler had no use for a worthless classical education. He wanted to toughen up young Germans and prepare them for the practical demands the regime would make on them.

I couldn't quite follow all this. I had cramps in my stomach, and my underpants once again felt a little moist.

He went on to explain that the students here were grouped into several "homes," each of which was assigned to a special sphere, such as patrol duty, navy, air force, communications, and motorized Hitler Youth. It was most unfortunate, he said, that I would not qualify for the SS division because I didn't have blond hair and my 5' 2" (160 cm) height did not meet the minimum height requirements. The *Bannführer*'s final words stunned me. Since I had already fought so bravely at the front at such a young age, he said, he was quite sure that I would become a Hitler Youth member who would be fully dedicated to his Führer and his people.

Before leaving the *Bannführer*'s office, I had to muster all my strength to raise my arm again in the obligatory Hitler salute. My mother's last words to me were now ringing in my ears, "You must live, you must live!" and it was only thanks to those words that I did not faint dead away, then and there.

The Hitler Youth was the third leg of a bloody triangle: SS, SA, HJ. In my mind's eye, I could still see their blood-thirsty faces before me as they pounced on Jews and opponents of the regime, wielding their daggers engraved with the words "Blood and Honor." And now I was one of them!

My immediate superior, *Heimführer* [Home Leader] Karl R., showed me my new accommodations in Home No. 7 of the Technical Service. I told him that I was very pleased with everything and that I was happy to exchange the difficult conditions at the front for these quarters. His only comment was that the grounds were indeed beautiful, that the main building had only recently been constructed in the New German style chosen by the Führer himself, and that it was a privilege to be one of the students in this unique school.

The facade of Home No. 7 was impressive. Its grandiose entrance hall was used as a reading room. Various newspapers lay about on rectangular tables, and the shelves along the walls were stocked with innumerable books. The office of the home leader was at the far end of the hall; to the right was a broad corridor from which the rooms branched off. This corridor led to the bathrooms and toilets. To the left of the reading room a flight of stairs led to the upper floor. A poster on one wall, printed in old-fashioned German Gothic letters, carried Hitler's exhortation to German youth: "Be hard as Krupp steel, tough as leather, and swift as a greyhound." The home leader showed me to my room and suggested I get settled in. "Relax for a while," he said, "and then come see me in my office."

My room was the second one on the right; it was spacious and functional. There were two beds, two armoires, two desks, and two chairs. At this hour the other rooms were

The Hitler Youth installation, Brunswick.

empty. On the wall over my bed was a motto about how "the purity of German blood" was being preserved primarily in the rural farm areas.

I put my things in a corner of the room, closed my eyes, and breathed deeply. In the oppressive silence I could hear my heart beat.

Oh Lord, what's going to become of me? I thought. What kind of survival have you prepared for me? Should I laugh or should I cry? No, I certainly won't cry. But I need courage, courage! Whatever happens, I have to forget little Solomon and start becoming a Hitler Youth, a genuine Josef.

Calmly I unpacked my things, putting everything neatly into the empty closet, everything except the bottle of French cognac I had brought with me. I wanted to give that to the home leader. I knew that alcoholic beverages, especially of such good quality, were practically unobtainable here. Perhaps a gesture like that would prompt him to respect me and that would help me get used to this place.

I sat down on the bed for a moment to rest a little and collect my thoughts. Suddenly a powerful curiosity prompted me to look into the bathrooms and toilets. Of course, I knew that I couldn't take showers with the other students, but the very thought made me tremble. I wanted to inspect the facilities before the others returned.

A pleasant surprise was in store for me, and my fears proved to have been exaggerated. The shower stalls were separated by frosted glass. This was reassuring. On the other hand, I didn't like the dressing room very much. I would have to get undressed and dressed alongside the others. How best to avoid the danger?

The toilets were as I had imagined them and seemed to present no problems. I went into one cubicle and bolted the door behind me. It was clean and gleamed as if it were new. On one wall someone had tried to quote Goethe: "Don't let anything bother you, remember the words of Götz von Berlichingen: ' . . . tell the King, he can kiss my ass!' "

I re-read the sentence, and as I walked out into the hall, I decided I would take that advice to heart from now on. In my happy frame of mind, I wished the others would too.

During my short life I had already learned to adapt and to overcome unexpected difficulties. Having succeeded at passing for a brave front-line fighter, I felt I could also solve the circumcision problem. I would become an exemplary member of the Hitler Youth.

Back in my room, I prepared for the interview with the home leader. I reviewed my concocted life history and decided to spice it up a little with a mixture of truth and inventive lies. Then I grabbed the bottle of cognac and made my way to the office of Home Leader Karl R. While I was still out in the corridor, I heard men laughing inside the office. They seemed to be in a good mood. I lingered a moment to catch my breath and to collect myself. I was about to come before not only my immediate superior but also some men I did not know who, I felt intuitively, were dangerous.

Transferring the bottle to my left hand so as to have my right hand ready for the Hitler salute, I knocked on the door. When I heard Karl R. call out, "Yes, come in," I confidently walked in and gave the proper salute. Then I smiled, proudly held out the bottle, and said, "I brought you a superb French cognac, a gift from my regiment at the front."

"Good Lord," said the home leader, "we have to get rid of that immediately. You should know that alcohol and tobacco are absolutely forbidden in our organization. The Führer, our supreme role model, doesn't smoke or drink." I quickly covered my dismay with an embarrassed smile and put the spurned bottle in a far corner of the room. Behind me someone whispered, "Oh well, that's not really so terrible; I heard he was a soldier."

The home leader asked me to take a seat. Other home leaders sat facing me. When I came in, they had interrupted their loud conversation to stare at me. Their brown uniforms and faultlessly tied black ties were decorated with various sports and party badges. I was particularly fascinated by their broad, black, swastika-emblazoned armbands. I managed to keep my self-control, and no one noticed that I was afraid, more afraid than I had been when I had to deal with senior *Wehrmacht* officers. It was obvious that these people had complete trust in the ideology in whose name they were committing their crimes against humanity. They considered these criminal acts to be patriotic missions in the interest of a greater Germany.

Karl R. told the group that I was the ethnic German they had just been talking about and that I had been sent back from the front by the *Wehrmacht*. There was a salvo of questions. I gave concise answers that seemed to satisfy them. Of course, I said nothing of the cynicism that was beginning to spread among the soldiers before I left, giving rise to remarks like, "It makes me want to throw up, Major, to see the entire front lines falling apart!" Nor did I mention anything about the first visible signs indicating that the *Blitzkrieg* was failing. Here they were still full of admiration for Hitler's genius as a military strategist. This blindness was to last until the very end of the war in May 1945. Even the frightful German defeat at Stalingrad didn't open their eyes. In any case, my protective mechanism had once again functioned smoothly.

Two contradictory voices were clashing within me: one constantly warning of the monstrous danger I was in; the other soothing and minimizing my dread, to the point of veiling it and making me forget it completely. Generally it was the latter that won out.

Solomon, alias Jupp the soldier, alias Josef the Hitler Youth, had found an ideal disguise behind which he could live in safety. But for how long? Could I, a circumcised Jew, go on like this forever, using a borrowed identity, without identification papers, while a mad, despotic regime summoned up every possible means to keep anything foreign from its people?

We went on talking for quite a while. After listening to my detailed account of events at the eastern front, the other home leaders left to go back to work. I stayed behind with Karl R. And then something unexpected happened. "Well now, Josef," he said, "let's have some of your cognac; it's only proper for a couple of front-line soldiers like us." He set out two glasses and a box of cookies. Amazed at this sudden turnabout, I fetched the bottle from the corner of the room where I had put it and poured some of the cognac into the glasses. We toasted each other's health. This was a portent of the good relationship we would have in the future, and from then on we were bound by a common secret: no one must find out that we had had a drink together in a model Hitler Youth school.

I had told Karl R. and the other home leaders the fabricated story of my life. Now he told me a little about himself. Until recently he had been an officer on active duty with the Waffen-SS. In 1940 he had lost a leg while fighting in France. (He struck the prosthesis with his fist; you couldn't mistake the sound it made.) After he recovered, he was offered several jobs, and he chose this one.

Forty years later, I would meet him again at his house in Brunswick.

I hadn't been back to Germany since the end of the war. Then, in November 1985, the mayor of Peine invited me to be the guest of honor at the dedication ceremony of a memorial to commemorate the destruction of the Peine synagogue, which was burned down on Kristallnacht, the Night of Shattered Glass. The invitation was extended to me as a Jew born in Peine who had survived the Holocaust. They didn't know the story of how *I survived. And so, with mixed feelings, I accepted.*

The ceremony included a torchlight procession, led by members of a youth club, to the site of the former synagogue. How I used to love going there with my father, especially on Simchas Torah, *the Jewish holiday on which children are pelted with candy and nuts.*

The street signs on what used to be Bodenstetter Strasse had been repainted in red. The street was now called Hans Marburger Strasse. Was this the same Hans Marburger who used to be my childhood friend, whose house adjoined ours, and who often played with me? I asked one of the men in the procession about that. He was, he said, the nephew of the former secretary of the local Communist party who had been murdered by the Nazis, and he told me a heart-wrenching story. On Kristallnacht, *he said, three Storm Troopers had forced their way into the Marburgers' house and started beating up Hans's father. Hans, showing incredible courage, tried to defend his father. The Storm Troopers immediately seized the boy, threw him into their car, and drove to the synagogue. There, after he was tied hand and foot, they locked him* up in the sanctuary. The synagogue burned to the ground, and Hans Marburger perished. His "crime" was trying to defend his father against the SA thugs. He was fifteen years old. Blessed be his memory.

It may at first seem incomprehensible, but that day I also looked up my former Hitler Youth home leader, Karl R. Having just been told about this monstrous, inhuman deed, how could I justify my meeting with a man who was a representative of such barbarity?

I offer no defense for my willingness to see him; perhaps life itself can do that. Sometimes the personality and character of a person are reason enough.

Occasionally the natural tendency to seek revenge gives way to generosity. A handshake does not necessarily signify forgiveness; on the contrary, it can express a generosity of mind and heart, a mixture of contempt and human triumph over hatred and atrocity.

But to get back to the events that led to my meeting with Karl R. During a brief speech at the memorial ceremony I told the audience, especially the young people there, the story of young Hans. I praised his exceptional bravery. He had not hesitated to come to his father's defense, I said, even though his chances were zero.

The next day the editors of the local newspaper interviewed me. During a lively conversation over coffee, one of the journalists wanted to know how I had survived the war. "I spent most of the time near here in Brunswick," I said. "I looked like a German, and I hid in the ranks of the Hitler Youth. I even strolled around Peine in uniform, right under the windows of your newspaper."

Judging from the surprised expressions on their faces and the skeptical looks they exchanged, the journalists didn't fully believe me. So I added some details. Apparently that dispelled their doubts. One of them asked, "Have you been back to Brunswick since then?" I said no, I hadn't.

"Would you go there with me?" he asked. "Perhaps we'll run into someone you knew there, maybe the home leader you told us about?" Having smelled a good story, he was insistent.

After thinking it over carefully I agreed, even though I still had reservations. I couldn't foresee the consequences such a meeting might have for me. I would be confronting the past, again creating a direct connection with what had been—a past that I had made such great efforts to suppress and that I did not want to touch. I would be allowing the dormant Jupp to come to life again and release thoughts that belonged only to me and no one else, and that I wanted to take to the grave with me. I had hoped to conceal these thoughts deep within me because I felt they were too vulnerable and too complex to entrust to others who might judge me too severely.

It took only twenty minutes to travel forty years into the past. Here were the once-familiar streets and buildings of Brunswick. I still knew how to get to the HJ school at 180 Gifhorner Strasse; it wasn't far. But now, as I stood there, I rubbed my eyes in amazement. Had memory played a trick on me? The main building, an expression of grandiose Hitlerian Machtarchitektur *[power architecture] was gone; there were no dormitories, no lawns or sport areas, no swimming pool or dining hall—instead it was all wasteland. The Volkswagen plant adjacent to the school had expanded to where the school used to be. The only remnant of all that had once been there was the classroom building, which now contained the technical offices of the auto factory. For three years I had gone into that building to study National Socialist racial doctrines, among other subjects. Everything that had been part of our everyday lives—the places where we ate, slept, engaged in sports, and so on—had been destroyed.*

Karl R.'s house was near the school. Sometimes I used to go for walks in that neighborhood. But we were in for a disappointment. His apartment was occupied by people who knew nothing about the tenants who had lived there in the forties.

We asked an elderly lady who was crossing the street, and she remembered Karl, "the disabled veteran." She told us that he had started a new venture, making dentures and false teeth, but she didn't know where he lived. Using a phone book at her house, we found what we were looking for.

I dialed Karl's number. His wife answered. Without telling her my name, I said I was one of her husband's former students and asked if I could see him so that we could share old memories. "Oh," she said, "Karl will be happy to see you. He just went out, but he'll be back in a few minutes. Please come over."

We wrote down the address and started out. From far away I recognized Karl standing at his front door. I knew that this meeting would lead me down paths I did not actually ever want to set foot on again. I felt horror and disgust, but also a sort of vague attraction. And then I was standing before him.

"Welcome, Jupp," he said, obviously moved. "How are you? What brings you here?" I was not smiling as we shook hands.

"Karl," I said, "I have something to tell you. My name isn't Josef Perjell; it's Solomon Perel and I am Jewish."

He didn't understand, even when the journalist accompanying me confirmed what I had just said. Karl looked at him, then at me, and turned pale. Gradually the enormity of a fact he wouldn't have dared imagine in his wildest dreams dawned on him. He was confused and upset. But finally he hugged me, saying softly, "Oh God, oh God, how wonderful to see you. . . ."

It was a spontaneous expression of genuine joy. I didn't want to play the role of avenger, although I was determined not to forget the past. I merely wanted to set the record straight. Still, this was a very warm human encounter, and I gave in to my emotions. We both cried.

But to get back to my story. After I left the home leader's office, giving the customary Hitler salute, I went to the clothing depot to pick up the uniform and equipment of a Hitler Youth.

On the heels of that dreadful trip, the tormenting uncertainty, the ever-present brown-shirted uniforms, and my grim prospects for the future, this seemed to be a promising beginning. I quickly learned to put up with things, to keep my wits about me, to suppress my fear, and always to act self-assured.

Completely relaxed, I walked into the uniform stock-
room where two not-so-young women were waiting for me.
I said hello, they answered with *"Heil."* Reluctantly, I
replied, *"Heil Hitler!"* One of them asked whether I was the
boy who had come back from the eastern front. I said yes,
realizing that here too my reputation had preceded me.
They laid out various items on a broad counter: complete
summer and winter outfits, two briefcases, field and work
clothes, socks, and shoes. One of the women put a belt and a
Hitler Youth dagger next to my pile of clothes; on the dagger
the inscription "Blood and Honor" made me shudder and I
flinched from taking it. Weren't those the very knives used
against Jews and opponents of the regime?

"Try on the belt," one of the women said. "Let's see if it
fits or whether you need a different size." I pulled myself together and buckled the belt around my waist.

Loaded down with things that belonged to the Third
Reich, I went back to my room, put everything onto the bed,
and—full of curiosity—slipped into my new uniform. I
wanted to take a look in the mirror, wanted to know what I
looked like in this outfit. To tell the truth, I wanted to greet
Jupp, the neophyte Hitler Youth.

The bed was freshly made; the sheets and blankets were
blue-and-white checkered. Again I looked at the framed slogan on the wall which in Gothic letters proclaimed that the
peasantry would keep German blood pure, and I thought,
Indeed! Wasn't I, as von Münchow's adopted son, also des-
tined to become a German farmer owning his own farm?
Then what would happen to your racial purity?

The home leader, smiling politely, put his head in the
door and told me that it was time for the evening meal. I was
to put on my field uniform, and then we would all march in
formation into the dining room. I finished putting things
away and went to take a quick shower before the others came
back. After hastily taking off my clothes in the farthest cor-

ner of the changing room, I jumped into the shower stall. I still had a bar of wonderful scented soap from Estonia that made lots of foam. At that moment, Jupp's spirits were high. He felt like singing his favorite aria from *I Pagliacci*, the one where Leoncavallo's clown weeps and laughs at the same time.

But it wasn't long before the shower, usually a place of relaxation and well-being, turned into one of frightening danger for me. When the soap I had brought with me was used up, I had to make do with the only soap there was in all of Germany. Called RIF soap, it had a disgusting smell and made almost no foam. This upset me inordinately, and I had to rub like crazy to get it to foam at all.

To hide my circumcision, I followed a simple but effective procedure. I undressed in next to no time but kept my underpants on; then I hopped right into the shower and, after closing the door behind me, finished undressing. I then made enough foam to cover the "dangerous body part" so that no one who might accidentally look in would see that the newcomer Jupp was circumcised.

Still, I felt that things could change from one moment to the next. So, when the others were there, I always withdrew to the farthest corner of the dressing room, to avoid their curious glances. Even today I still have a feeling of anxiety and a stomachache when I go into the common shower at my athletic club.

When I met Karl R. again, he suddenly remembered that several of my classmates had come to see him in those days to tell him of my peculiar behavior in the dressing room. Now they may finally find out what caused it. . . .

The RIF soap created a paradoxical situation. I would swear at the soap because it didn't make enough foam, and the others would call it the "damned Jew-soap." RIF, they said, stood for *Reines Judenfett* [pure Jewish fat]. Our curses were directed toward the same soap, but what a difference there was between their reasons and mine! Since I had learned how important it was to keep my feelings under control no matter what, I never tried to find out what the soap's initials really stood for.

Some years ago, on the day commemorating the Shoah, Israeli television interviewed a Jew who was holding a bar of RIF in his hand. He explained that he had brought the soap to Israel to bury it, since it consisted of drops of fat from the bodies of thousands of Jews. Hearing him say this was a difficult ordeal for me. So far, his claim has not been substantiated.

The circumcision problem, an almost insuperable obstacle, tormented me constantly. And so I decided to perform a "do-it-yourself operation": I would stretch the foreskin.

While visiting a friend who was in the League of German Girls [BDM—*Bund Deutscher Mädel*], I saw a ball of thick, soft wool lying on her table. She was knitting a sweater for the winter. This yarn was just right for what I wanted to do, and I stuffed a few inches of it into my pocket.

Back in school, I locked myself in the toilet and got to work. I pulled my foreskin firmly down, cursing the *mohel* who had performed the circumcision for not having been more generous. I wrapped the foreskin with the woolen threads to keep it from slipping back and shrinking to its original size. Because the skin was so elastic I hoped that after a few days it would stretch permanently and stay in place.

Recently I found out that I wasn't the first one to have tried such a cover-up operation. Hellenized Jews had pulled down their foreskins in order to obliterate the last vestige of their Jewishness. But at the time I was conducting my experiment, I didn't even know these ancient people had ever existed.

I walked around bandaged like that for a few days. During every break I hurried to the toilet, my "treatment room," to see how things were going and if necessary to make adjustments. Even during the night, I checked to see whether my foreskin was still tied properly. But after a few days, I gave up. A painful inflammation had set in, and I had to remove the woolen threads.

Although I could barely walk, I did my work as usual. During the daily marching drill I was painfully reminded of my unsuccessful manipulation. I was in charge of a group of fourteen-year-old boys, and one of them asked me, "Josef, why don't you stand up straight when you march and why don't you keep in step?" Finding excuses had become second nature to me, and so I promptly answered, "Oh, it's nothing; my back hurts."

"Why don't you report to sick bay?" the little pest asked.

"I will, if it doesn't get better in a day or two. You don't run to the doctor for every little thing."

He nodded.

My answer enhanced the younger boys' respect for me. But what was I to do? In whom could I confide? To go to the doctor would have been like saying, "I surrender. You've won. I'm yours. Kill me." But suicide never tempted me, and under the circumstances it didn't seem an appropriate solution. Hadn't Mama ordered me to stay alive?

I had hoped that the "treatment" would prove successful. But sometimes the higher one's hopes, the deeper the disappointment. The skin shrank back again; my problem hadn't gone away.

I remembered a conversation I once overheard. Some front-line soldiers were talking about penises. One of them explained that nature had given the male sex organ extraordinary self-healing properties; thanks to a layer of fat under the skin, any wound or inflammation heals quickly. Recalling this bit of hygienic wisdom now, I decided just to wait things out. To my great relief and joy, I found that the soldier was right. Without any treatment the inflammation began to fade and eventually it disappeared completely.

I celebrated my recovery with a few sips of the liqueur I had kept in secret reserve. Not ever again, I vowed, would I mess with the *mohel's* work!

I had never held it against my parents that they initiated me into the Covenant of Abraham, the patriarch of our people. That was taken for granted, just as my name Solomon was, and the fact that I had this particular face and not another. Nor did I want to deny or reject my origins. But I knew that I had to find some solution for my identity problem until these dark times were over, to hold out until we were free again. The faith and the certainty that I would not be in this place forever sustained me.

On that first day in the Hitler Youth school I had taken a shower and, in a good mood, I returned to my room dressed in my new uniform. How often had I heard the old saying, "Appearances are deceptive." In my case this certainly seemed to be true. I had carefully and calmly put on that dreadful uniform and, standing in front of the mirror, I had asked myself, "Shloimele, is that really you?" Sadness and horror briefly flitted across my face, then I smiled at my reflection, thinking, I've been lucky so far, and I'll go on being lucky!

Hitler Youth Jupp and Solomon the Jew got along like fire and water. Still, they existed side by side in the same body, in the same mind.

Just then I heard voices in the hall, coming closer. With my heart pounding, I put on a serious expression. What kind of people would these young men be? Most of them had straw-blond hair; how would they react to my appearance? What sort of person would my roommate be?

The door opened, and he walked in. As I had expected, he was blond and good-looking, but he had the face of a spoiled child. Surprised to see a stranger in his room, he stopped in his tracks, and greeted me with *"Heil Hitler!"* I smiled and introduced myself as the new student. Then I gave him a brief summary of the life story I had made up for myself. He introduced himself as Gerhard R. and told me how pleased he was to share the room with me.

This fellow won't create any trouble for me, I thought; we'll get along. Our conversation was interrupted by the voice of the *Scharführer* [comparable to a staff sergeant] in the hall: "Get ready to march to the dining hall in five minutes!" I would be marching with them, wearing their uniform and their shoes. My steps would pound just as loudly on the floorboards, marching in time to the left-right, left-right of the infamous goose step that was crushing Europe and making the entire world tremble.

After I put away the last of my things, Gerhard and I left the room. In the hall we joined the other students pouring out of their rooms. Some gave me curious looks. Gerhard explained to those who stood next to him that I was a new student and that I had come to the school straight from the fighting front. He didn't know what an inestimable service he was doing me. At this, my first meeting with the others, my trump card was already on the table: I was the *Wehrmacht* volunteer, the famous front-line fighter! In the years I was to spend with them, they would always make allowances because of my war record.

Each of the boys knew what he was supposed to do, and they quickly formed rows of four. The *Scharführer* asked me not to line up with them, not yet, but to wait until the home leader arrived. I sensed that the first impression I made would be decisive.

When the home leader arrived, he pointed to me, identified me by name and mentioned my German origins so that everybody could hear. Then he gave a detailed account of my military history and emphasized that the commander of my unit had sent me here so that I could continue my education and learn more about my fatherland. Therefore, all students were under orders to be helpful to me. Of course, I knew that all this talk about my contribution to the Russian campaign, about the bravery that I, who was not much more than a child, had shown, about my readiness to sacrifice my life for my Führer and my people, was just stupid, hollow words. Only the devil could think up such inanities. But given my emotional distress, these words of encouragement were like balm to a wounded soul.

I must admit that pretty soon I began to believe my own web of lies and to identify with it.

"Right, right, forward march!" the *Scharführer* barked. I was ordered to bring up the rear.

Yes, it's true, I fell in with their steps . . . I adapted to their marching tempo. . . .

Without any instructions, they spontaneously and enthusiastically started to sing. I knew these songs: "*Auf der Heide wächst ein Blümelein, das heisst Erika*" [A flower grows on the heath, it's called heather] and "*Die Lorelei,*" and under my breath I hummed along.

But then I stopped and listened more carefully. They were singing a song I had never heard before:

Die Juden zieh'n dahin, daher
Sie zieh'n durchs Rote Meer
Die Wellen schlagen zu
Die Welt hat Ruh'.

The Jews, they wander here and there
They're marching through the Red Sea
The waves close over them
At last the world's at peace.

They still hadn't forgiven God for the Exodus from Egypt, for having led his children dry-shod through the sea instead of drowning them. As we approached the dining hall, they started a new song with horrendous murderous verses: *"Erst wenn vom Messer spritzt das Judenblut, dann geht's uns nochmal so gut"* [We'll be even better off once Jewish blood spurts from our knives].

They were singing this song on their way to a well-set table. Would I be able to touch the food after this?

Something terrible, a barbaric inhuman odium, clung to this song. The tramping of German hobnailed boots could be heard far and wide. Millions of terrorized people were fleeing before them. The words of another of their songs heralded occupation and destruction: *"Wir werden weiter marschieren, bis alles in Scherben fällt / Heute gehört uns Deutschland und morgen die ganze Welt"* [We will march onward until everything is destroyed / Today Germany is ours, tomorrow the whole world].

Marching to this powerful rhythm, we arrived at the dining hall. The pride and joy of the school, it could accommodate up to a hundred students. There were paintings of Viking heroes, flaming swastikas, guns, flowers, and plows on the walls. Nobody sat down right away. They were all standing stiff and straight as pokers, their eyes directed toward a small gallery below the high ceiling at the front of the hall. There, behind a microphone, sat the home leader getting ready to speak. Solemnly he waited until the last whisper had died down. I wondered what sort of prayer they were going to say. Out of the corner of my eye I glanced at the boy next to me so that I could immediately copy his every gesture and lip movement.

A deathly silence reigned. And then the home leader spoke; the acoustics of the hall, which were comparable to those of a cathedral, amplified his voice. The song about "Jewish blood spurts from our knives" still rang in my ears, so it was difficult to concentrate, to understand what he was saying. After a while, I picked up a few words: "Keep the

race pure . . . be strong . . . *Lebensrecht* [right to life]. . . ." I
thought, It's nothing but Nazi jargon.

What I couldn't know was that in the next three years I
would be learning and teaching these same ideas.

He came to the end of his talk and said he hoped we'd
enjoy our meal. We began to eat. We were served hot vege-
table soup, rolls, cheese, and artificial honey. For dessert
there was tea.

Gerhard, who was sitting next to me, was the first to talk
to me. He could scarcely contain his curiosity, and he said,
loud enough for the others to hear, "Come on, describe it.
What was the war like where you were?" I wanted to tell him
to go to hell, to leave me alone. I was very tired. But, of
course, I didn't. Instead I started to talk about the various
battles and the life of the soldiers fighting the war against
"Jewish Bolshevism." I was at the top of my form as a story-
teller, and I held them spellbound. My military service
record, issued by the commander of the "glorious 12th
Panzer Division," lent credibility to my stories. The desig-
nation on the document that it was signed on the order of an
active-duty general officer allowed for no skepticism. I
avoided exaggerations, since I knew how they all looked up
to war heroes.

An hour after we finished eating, I was still sitting at the
center of a group of boys who had gathered around me. I answered their questions and described in detail all the adventures and ordeals my division had experienced. Their
mouths were literally hanging open. And these fellows, all
urban youths and generally well educated, were neither stupid nor particularly naive. But they had been subjected to
regular brainwashing, had been infused with the poison of a
corrupted science, and their love of their fatherland had
been turned into fanaticism. They had been converted into
devout followers of Adolf Hitler, and they were devoted to
this false prophet, body and soul. Any original ideas, any

critical spirit, had been driven out of them. Blindly, they followed the principle "Führer, command us, we will obey!"

Nazi policy demanded unconditional obedience to one's superiors. There was no room for discussion. One had no choice. The majority of the people did not voice their opinions. Only the leaders at various levels made decisions, which their subordinates would then put into action without protest.

I was greatly relieved when the conversation petered out. We dispersed, each going to his room, even though there was a social function that evening and a meeting was taking place in the lecture hall. Well, well, Shloimele, I thought. You won't get bored here!

Back in our room, Gerhard sat down at his desk and opened his notebooks. Luckily, my group was excused from duty that night, and so for the first time I had an opportunity to lie down on my bed and rest.

Upstairs, another group of students was preparing posters and publicity material for a procession that was to march through the streets of Brunswick accompanied by the school band to inform people about possible air raids. Residents would be asked to clean out their air raid shelters and to outfit them with fire extinguishers and first aid kits for emergencies.

I often went to the reading room to check the newspapers for developments at the front. One day there were numerous black-bordered obituaries; each one bore an Iron Cross symbol. And in each, the same phrase was repeated: "He died on the field of honor for his Führer, his People, and his Fatherland.—The bereaved family." According to the news reports, everything was fine at the front, and the enemy allegedly was retreating after sustaining heavy losses. The papers quoted excerpts from Hitler's latest hysterical public speech. He blindly claimed that the *Wehrmacht* was encountering no setbacks in its occupation of Holland, Belgium, Norway, and other European countries. "Even Stalingrad is ours and will remain so . . . !" And, of course, there were photographs of thousands of his followers enthusiastically cheering their Führer at mass meetings.

Later, in February 1943, there would be a three-day period of mourning throughout the Reich because the German Sixth Army, under its supreme commander, Field Marshal Friedrich Paulus, had been annihilated by the Red Army.

I also came across a brief item, on the inside pages, about the so-called Madagascar plan. According to this article, all Jews were to be driven out of Europe so that it could become *judenrein* [cleansed of Jews].

I felt no joy when I subsequently read about the Russian victory at Stalingrad, and the article about the planned expulsion of the Jews to the African island of Madagascar did not upset me inordinately. It seemed I had worked out a compromise, a sort of mental balance, between Jupp and Solomon. I had fused the two selves into a new personality that was not vulnerable to external provocations and inner conflicts. I tried not to think of the implications of the Madagascar decree. I felt it simply didn't concern me, and so I didn't allow it to affect me personally. I couldn't and didn't want to imagine my parents among those who were to be expelled.

The secret workings of a shattered soul are sometimes unfathomable. And so I continued to believe that a guardian angel was controlling my destiny. At no time did I make an attempt to dispute this or to rebel against him. He was not a god in the religious sense; he was my personal god, my private god, in whom I believed. I certainly was not about to oppose anything that was laid down by this higher power.

My attention was drawn to *Die Fanfare*, a beautifully illustrated Hitler Youth magazine published monthly by our local HJ *Bann* 468. I picked it up and began to leaf through

A snowball fight with my Hitler Youth comrades, Brunswick, winter
1942. I am on the right.

it. In addition to news items about the school orchestra and various workshops, there were appeals to the students to write letters to soldiers at the front, to give them moral support, to assure them that their fatherland loved them, and to emphasize the students' belief in Germany's ultimate victory. That prompted me to write to my old unit and to Captain von Münchow in order to find out how they were getting along and whether anyone had been killed in action.

By now, Solomon had turned into Josef the Hitler Youth, and I felt a special need to keep in touch with those men, who really should have been my deadly enemies but to whom I was instead linked by a common destiny. Their constant concern for my welfare when I had been with them, and the danger we had all faced of being killed and buried on foreign soil, bound me to them. I still remember how hard they had tried to find a remedy for the excruciating knee pains that I suffered at one time. Neither Heinz's painkiller pills nor the other medicines had worked. But one of the soldiers had finally relieved my suffering.

He slashed the bark of several birch branches and collected the thick sap that ran out. I applied this resin to my knees several times, and the pain disappeared miraculously, as though it had never existed. I'm not sure that it was the birch sap that cured me, but it was reassuring to know that another human being, who wasn't personally involved, should care about me.

Since my life was in constant danger, these small gestures were like rays of sunshine falling into the profound gulf that separated us. I hated the Nazi regime and rejected it completely, and yet I was well disposed toward these men. Despite my fervent prayers for their quick defeat and for the rescue of my family and my fellow Jews, I felt a remarkable affection for them. This must be completely incomprehensible to someone who sees things from a one-dimensional perspective.

4

Hitler Youth Perjell

When I came back to my room that first night, Gerhard was already in bed, reading a book. A few minutes later, so was I. Taking a deep breath, I asked Gerhard, more out of politeness than anything else, "Where are you from?"

"My hometown is very close by," he answered. "I'm from Peine."

I wanted to jump out of bed and exclaim with delight, "What an incredible coincidence! I'm from Peine too." But that would have destroyed my whole fragile structure of lies and any hope of staying alive. I would have been pronouncing my own death sentence. Since all could be lost with a single slip of the tongue, any spontaneous expression of feelings was out of the question. So I pretended ignorance and asked, "Where is Peine?"

"Oh, it's not far from here," he explained, "maybe twelve miles from Brunswick. I'll invite you to my house one of these Sundays. I'm sure my parents would be happy to meet you. And that will give you a chance to do some sightseeing in town." Our conversation, so full of pitfalls for me, ended when I said, "Thank you. Good night."

I tossed and turned, hoping to fall asleep. But I kept wondering about the future and what it had in store for me. If Gerhard had seen me at that moment, he would have noticed the worried expression on my face and he probably would have thought there was something suspect about his new roommate. Luckily, his face was turned toward the ceiling.

Despite all this, I woke up the next day thinking, Hello, Germany! Good morning, school! I slept very well in your bed this first night. It was a refreshing sleep from which no bad dream roused me.

From all indications, Hitler Youth Jupp felt quite comfortable in his new role, in contrast to Shloimele, who had had to dry his bedsheets on the clothesline outside the orphanage in Grodno. Jupp fitted in completely with these "elite" young Germans. He had suppressed his memories of Solomon and was trying to forget the past—yet he was doing this only to save the life of Shloimele Perel, Azriel and Rebecca's son, grandson of a wise man from Wilkomir and grandson also of Reb Eliahu Bar Halperin. Deep down, from time to time, he remembered all this; the spark of his origin was not, and would never be, extinguished.

The spring sun was shining. An intoxicating fragrance from the lawns and flowerbeds came through the open windows. I got up and looked at my new world. The beauty of the landscape strengthened my resolve, and I vowed to let nothing discourage me until we could celebrate the triumph of life and freedom.

On my way to the washrooms I hummed the familiar melody of "Lili Marlene." Smiling politely, I returned the "Good morning" and "*Heil*" of everyone I met. Then I carefully put on my uniform. It had been ironed to perfection, as was fitting, for the morning march to our *Kraft durch Freude* temple. The Nazis had written the word *Kraft* [strength] on their flags and renamed the neighboring town of Wolfsburg KdF-Stadt [Strength-through-Joy City]. That's where the main plant of Volkswagen was located. We would be going there soon as part of the convoluted course our lives were taking.

After a delicious breakfast, I had an unexpected and enjoyable chat with the home leader. My inner tension of two days before had begun to fade.

The breakfast had included some of that artificial honey, so similar in taste and color to natural honey you practically couldn't tell the difference. I liked it. Later someone told me that it was made from coal. The Germans used certain byproducts of the refineries to prepare this mineral-rich, edible "honey." Now I could more fully appreciate the stickers next to the light switches. They showed a caricature of a scoundrel with a soot-blackened face wearing an eye-patch and carrying a sack of coal slung over his back. The inscription warned, "Don't be a coal thief. Save energy. Turn off the light."

That morning I was told to go to see Miss Köchy in the main office. My old stomach cramps came back. What did they want this time? I made my bed, and while the other boys in the house headed for their classes, I went to look for Miss Köchy in the building where I had first met the *Bannführer*. An impressive silence reigned there. Only a door closing now and then and the soft murmur of voices indicated that there were people present. To the right of the entry hall, on a white door marked with a red cross, there was a sign that said "Infirmary." I stopped in my tracks, and suddenly an icy shiver ran down my spine: a new danger—a physical examination—threatened. Why hadn't I thought of that before? Any fledgling doctor would immediately see my circumcision. I simply couldn't afford to get sick.

In Miss Köchy's office I introduced myself. I liked her smile and her kind manner. She was about twenty-five years old, wore glasses, and seemed pleasant but looked almost ugly and unfeminine. Later, like the other boys, I called her "Ironing Board" behind her back.

We have met several times since those days, and even today we feel affection and friendship for each other. She is still single, but better looking today than when she was young.

She asked me to sit down, and I was flattered to hear her say that she was impressed by my recent experience in the *Wehrmacht.* Her kind words calmed my fears.

I was less pleased when I found out why I had been asked to see her. Additional personal details were required for my file and for the psychological and technical tests I was scheduled to take. I had already heard of the HJ "workshops," but I didn't know what went on there. I was relieved when Miss Köchy explained: This school, set up in accordance with Hitler's ideas, was the first experiment of its kind in Germany. It combined political and scientific education with hands-on production work, which was being taught in the nearby Volkswagen plant.

I had become a master at the art of continually adding new details to my "life story," so this interview presented no particular difficulties for me. But there was one question she asked that hit me like a thunderclap: "Names and origin of your parents?" Even though I had already been asked that by the painstaking Captain von Münchow and had answered it right off the bat at that time, I now was momentarily thrown off balance. I blushed. The question unexpectedly pierced the thick shell behind which I had taken cover. Without moving my lips, I murmured, "Mama, Papa, . . . where are you?" Bitter tears came to my eyes. "I'm sorry, I can't give you an answer. I was brought to the orphanage when I was still very little. I never saw my parents. . . . I am all alone."

She did not try to conceal her sympathy as she entered these data into my file.

Once again I was amazed that such false details were simply accepted and written down without suspicion and without verification. Not one of the painfully meticulous officials at the various police stations, the Gestapo, or Internal Security had made an effort to follow up on the information I had given them by checking with the registry office in Grodno. I am still puzzled by the trust they placed in what I told them. Are those right who say that everything that will ever happen, from the very beginning to the end of a man's life, has been preordained?

Thank God, Miss Köchy did not notice my confusion. After that, our conversation continued smoothly. "Yes," I said, "I do speak some other languages—Russian and Polish." I didn't mention that I had also formally studied Yiddish grammar in Grodno. That was Solomon's secret treasure, and I kept it to myself.

And so I was admitted as a regular student to this unique Hitler Youth unit, *Bann* 468, Northern Lower Saxony, Brunswick.

Before Miss Köchy sent me to an adjoining room to take the psychological and technical tests, we exchanged a few additional polite words. As I left the room, I gave her a snappy Hitler salute. In a fascist, totalitarian regime you never knew what other people were thinking; that's why it was most advisable not to neglect these rituals. Being careless about such things might have clouded the image I wanted to project.

In the adjacent office I had to take apart a metal object and reassemble it within a limited time. I did my best because I knew that if I accomplished this without making any mistakes, I would be in clover. And that's what happened—I did very well, ranking with the best. They then gave me school supplies and several books I had heard about but never read. Among them were Hitler's *Mein Kampf* and *The Myth of the 20th Century* by Alfred Rosenberg, the chief ideologue of the Nazi party. In the three years that followed I read and re-read both these works, which were prominent in National Socialist ideology and created the bases for the Nazi racial theories.

The usual academic courses didn't give me any trouble; on the contrary, I found reassurance and satisfaction in that sort of work. I learned quickly and appreciated the importance of what I learned. (Years before, one of my teachers in Lodz had predicted that I would become a professor. In Grodno I had been one of those who excelled "in learning and discipline," with my photograph posted on the honor roll of the high school.) It was the lessons in "racial theory" that were the worst and most painful to endure.

Now, decades later, I have to try hard to recall the things I was forced to memorize in those days. To do this I have to shut myself off from the outside world, close my eyes, stroke my chin . . . and go back in time until I'm in the classroom again, sitting in my seat in the middle row. I have a stomachache, cramps, just as I did then. I am seventeen years old again, tensely sitting among the other students, wearing my swastika-adorned uniform, waiting. Soon the door will open and the Race Studies teacher will walk in. He is young, has short blond hair, and wears thin, gold-metal-rimmed eyeglasses. He wears a brown SA uniform and black boots. The students jump up, stand stiff-backed, raise their right arms, and yell as if with one voice, "*Heil Hitler!*" Then they sit down again, straining forward, silent, motionless, their eyes fixed on the teacher. The silence that drags on for minutes is unbearable. The air crackles with tension.

Calmly the teacher opens his textbook; slowly he looks around, checks attendance, makes some notes. And then the lesson begins.

The dogma he is espousing—all directed against my people—makes me want to scream. I remain in my seat, a prisoner; I wait impatiently for the bell to ring, to liberate me. During the break I keep to myself, trying to calm down before the next class.

How could I have sat there among them learning about laws that were meant to drain the lifeblood from the Jewish people? How did I keep my sanity? Perhaps I simply did not realize how loathsome the situation was in which I found myself. I suffered from chronic persecution anxiety. Whenever someone unexpectedly called my name, or if I was told to report to one of my superiors, it immediately triggered the alarming and terrible thought that my last hour had struck. Every stranger was a possible Gestapo officer, come to arrest me.

Almost all the things I was taught frightened and shocked me. One of the chapters in the textbook was titled "Characteristic and Distinguishing Features of Jews." The objective of the lesson was to teach us "how to recognize your enemy." On one of the walls of the classroom hung enlarged photographs of Jewish faces, in profile and full-face. There was also a drawing of "The Eternal Jew," a shrunken man leaning on a walking stick, wearing tattered clothes and carrying a pack of rags on his back. The caption said "This is how they came to Germany from the East. . . ." The next picture showed the same Jew, but this time he had a fat belly, was splendidly dressed, wore gold and diamond jewelry, and held a cigar between his craftily smiling lips. A German peasant was writhing beneath one of the Jew's feet. This time the caption read " . . . and this is what they became in our midst."

True to German thoroughness, every detail, every limb, and every conceivable type of skull were systematically examined in class. The list of distinguishing Jewish features got longer day by day and finally filled the entire blackboard. Industrious Jupp—who, after all, wanted to be a good student—copied everything down with a steady hand. Only his eyes glanced around furtively. Had anyone noticed anything strange about him? For I resembled many of the prototypes they showed us, and I had many of the "distinguishing Jewish features" that were described to us. We were told you could tell a Jew by his low forehead, his long skull, his stunted physique (in contrast to tall Aryans), the long hooked nose, the circumcision, flat feet, and so on. Once the teacher also mentioned Jewish body language, that is, the way Jews gesticulated. I immediately resolved that I would no longer emphasize my words with lively gestures. At least that would eliminate another possible cause for suspicion.

But one day I got some unexpected support that gave a boost to my morale. It happened at a lecture on "the ethnic nature of our community [*die völkische Beschaffenheit unserer Gemeinschaft*]." We had been told that "the alliance of German blood" was composed of six races; the master race that ranked above all others was the Nordic. Its descendants possessed characteristics that predestined them to power, organization, knowledge, and culture. The fact that God had given these characteristics only to the Nordic race proved that it, and only it, was the chosen race. Only it was able to create order in the world and, in particular, to save the West from collapse: "God has chosen us."

One of the primary aims of the Führer and the Nazi party was to hasten the expansion of the Nordic race. To do this they were prepared to include some other, less privileged races such as the Finns, West Europeans, Romanians, and people of the Eastern Baltic area with whom, because of the influence of foreign peoples and in the course of many generations, the Nordic element had become mixed. To push the "Germanization process" along—it had achieved cult status—they had brought over young men from Norway, who were first given a thorough physical examination. They were then brought together with pure Aryan women in establishments set up just for this purpose. There the women were permitted to have sexual intercourse with these carefully selected men. The fruit of these couplings was presented to the Führer as a symbol of the glorification of the Nordic race. For the most part, the newborns, called sun children [*Sonnenkinder*], were adopted by families of SS members or placed in National Socialist educational institutions.

Once, while I was sitting in a beer hall in Brunswick with a few friends, a couple of female students came over to join us. One of them proudly told us that a speaker from the Propaganda Ministry had come to her university campus. He had urged her to personally take part in carrying out the Führer's command to raise the birthrate of the Nordic race. He reminded her that the commandment "Be fruitful and multiply" was the highest law of the German *Volk* community. I didn't ask the young lady whether she had taken the chance to enjoy herself. Another girl I knew, a member of the League of German Girls [BDM], had made her womb available for this purpose without telling her parents.

According to the learned speaker from the Propaganda Ministry, the Norwegians were the only people who had pure Nordic blood in their veins, without any foreign admixture — a heritage of the old Teutons and Vikings.

Youths from all regions of the German Reich attended our school, pure Nordic types and students showing other racial traits. The teacher would call on us to come to the front of the classroom, one at a time. He would point out particular racial features and discuss them. One day, as I was sitting there deep in thought, I heard my name being called. Come to the front of the class, I was told. I began to tremble. What kind of nonsense had the young SA teacher hatched this time? What sort of show-and-tell was this going to be? I got up and went to the blackboard as though I were walking the plank over a deep abyss, as though I, an innocent spectator, were being sent into the arena with the gladiators. No retreat was possible, and—although I wished it—the earth didn't open up to swallow me. On the way to the blackboard I was amazed to see that my classmates were looking at me in a completely normal way, and the teacher also behaved just as he always did. He didn't seem to be contemplating an execution. I relaxed.

Then came the surprise! The teacher said, "Class, take a look at Josef. He is a typical descendant of the Eastern Baltic race." Heaven be praised! At this instant thousands of research projects by Nazi racial scholars reached a point of utter absurdity, their alleged scholarly competence uncovered for what it really was: zero! I smiled in embarrassment. What a boost for my morale. A proven man of science had handed me a superb report card. Suddenly I saw myself confirmed as an Aryan. Before this, on more than one occasion, I fancied they had given me mistrustful and surprised looks, but now I no longer saw my pitch-black hair and short stature as defects. Thank you for giving me new hope, you messenger from Satan's realm.

About two weeks after the end of the war I ran into this "worthy" former teacher at the train station in Hanover. His name was Borgdorf. I was on my way to visit the former concentration camp Bergen-Belsen, and suddenly I found myself face to face with him on a stairway. He said he was happy to see me and asked how I was and where I was going. "To Bergen-Belsen near Celle," I told him. "But first there's something I'd like to tell you. Do you remember how, in one of the Race Education classes, you—a great German scientist—singled me out as a typical representative of the Eastern Baltic race? Well, that was a mistake, and I'd like to correct it now. I am in no way a member of that race; nor am I an Aryan. I'm of pure Jewish blood, from head to toe!"

Obviously the man was a master at dissimulation. His face betrayed no emotion whatsoever. In fact, he tried once again to demonstrate his expertise by saying, "I knew it all along, but I was trying to avoid hurting you . . . !"

Since I'm not vindictive, I left him standing there and continued on my way.

Recently, while writing this account, I was able to recall more of the racial theory that I was taught in those days and that I thought I had forgotten.

According to our "outstanding" teacher, the geographic location of Germany in the center of Europe gave rise to constant conflicts with neighboring countries (this is historically correct). Consequently, Germany's existence and honor were threatened. The security of the German Reich could be assured only by the expansion of its military power. To win in battle, the German people had to be healthy and strong. They had to recognize the laws of nature and live in concert with them. And of course, the teacher told us, one fundamental law was the Law of Natural Selection. All species are in a constant struggle for survival. Plants fight one another for light. Wild animals attack one another to defend their territory and subsistence. A fledgling bird that can't fly is thrown out of the nest. . . .

According to this Law of Natural Selection, the survivor is the one who overpowers the others. Nature mercilessly weeds out everything that is weak and sick. The young National Socialist state decided to apply this law ruthlessly. It began by preventing the mating of the weak with the strong. Social welfare and charitable organizations, we were told, fostered the survival of weak and dim-witted individuals who did not contribute to the good of the people as a whole. According to our teacher, the alarming national deficit was caused by wasting money on the weak and the sick.

He also said that not only were physical traits inherited, but also psychological and mental ones, such as willpower and, at the other extreme, laziness. Therefore, sterilization of the genetically impaired elements of society would make it possible to, once and for all, eliminate mental illnesses, chronic diseases, deafness, blindness, physical handicaps, and so on.

In addition, he maintained, there was another unalterable natural law: living things reproduce only within the same species. An eagle does not mate with a raven, nor a tiger with a lioness. The existing exceptions—among mammals, for instance, a cross between a horse and a donkey— could be attributed to human intervention. But even in such cases Nature made its rules very clear by preventing such hybrids from reproducing. Nature was opposed to the mixing of species and punished hybrids by making them sterile.

Human beings, he said, are subject to the same principle. When they add foreign blood to their own strain, they are doomed, as demonstrated by the fall of the Greek and Roman civilizations. People of mixed blood exist in a schizophrenic condition. Their national traits and characteristics get mixed up, their thinking and emotions degenerate, and in the end they decline and produce inferior offspring. Therefore, the German people have to comply with Nature's laws; they must become hard and merciless.

I remember a slogan one of our teachers used in this connection: "We don't need scholars; we need defenders of the fatherland." And there was also the poster in our classroom that quoted the Führer: "Your body belongs to your national community; it is your duty to stay healthy."

We were also taught that it was a German tradition to keep our bloodline pure. For many generations the German race had remained inviolable. But then, in the nineteenth century, all the barriers had come down following the French Revolution, when the motto "Liberty, Equality, Fraternity" was adopted also by the German people. This paved the way for the mixing of blood, and it was primarily Jewish blood that was mixed with pure German blood.

Naturally, the teacher said, the Jews used this to carry out their plan to subjugate, enslave, and exploit the Aryan race. As proof of the alleged Jewish world conspiracy, copies of *Protocols of the Elders of Zion* were handed out in class, so that we could see for ourselves the devastating Jewish influence on politics, the economy, and culture. (The *Protocols* were a forgery, composed by agents of the Russian Czar, that purported to be a report of twenty-four secret sessions of the Elders of Zion in Switzerland in their conspiracy to conquer the world.) To make matters worse, we were told, the Jewish race was a mixture of Mongols, Asians, and blacks.

It was conceded that biologically the Jew resembled a human being, since he had a mouth, eyes, limbs, and something resembling a brain. But mentally and morally he was on a rung below the animals and was ruled by evil instincts. Furthermore, they told us, "The shamelessness of the Jew was increasing and would soon know no bounds." Therefore, nobody should be surprised that the German people regarded him as the devil incarnate.

In one of these classes our teacher read a shocking excerpt from *Der Stürmer*, a weekly paper started by Julius Streicher and dedicated to the vilification of the Jews. The paper reported that a young girl living in a German village had written a letter to her pastor in which she asked him, "Weren't the Jews also created in the image of God?"

The paper's reply to this girl's brave question was appalling: "You say that the Jews were also created in the image of God. To that we say: Nature also created bloodsucking vermin and disease-transmitting ticks. In order to protect the health of humanity, it is our duty to wipe the Jews off the map."

Is it then any wonder that the people who carried out the extermination of the Jews murdered children and babies in the belief that they were fulfilling a mission? This gruesome doctrine provided them with justification for their acts.

I sensed that I was gradually becoming ensnared by this depraved "science," or at least by some of its aspects. Eventually, I became convinced that a superior people had the right to rule, and that, in the interest of breeding a healthy and industrious nation, you could forbid the weak to reproduce, the idea being to prevent genetic disease. I neither questioned my belief in this ideology nor did it surprise me. Day by day Jupp remembered Solomon less and less.

One day the German love for procedural efficiency again called official attention to me. I was summoned to the VW plant office, and going there, I again visualized being interrogated and arrested, my final hour approaching. I began to panic. I had spent the last few weeks without a care, and now my house of cards threatened to collapse once more. But then my eternal optimism won out, and I convinced myself this whole thing probably was just a petty matter. The closer I got to the office, the more my trust in my lucky star suppressed the waves of fear. I talked myself into believing that nothing bad could happen to me. After all, other trials had come and gone, and each time I had come through with ease. My self-defense mechanisms had worked superbly up to now and they wouldn't let me down this time either.

At the office I reported to the woman in charge of personnel problems, who was also a BDM leader. The enthusiastic Hitler salute I gave her could have left no doubt where I stood. Since no Gestapo officers were there to drive me into a corner, I calmed down, relaxed a little, and stopped thinking about the tension of the preceding few minutes. Solomon's anxiety subsided, and Jupp took a deep breath.

"Are you Josef Perjell?" she asked.

"Yes indeed!" I replied.

"We received a court summons for you. You have to report to the clerk of the court as soon as possible. A routine matter."

"Do you know what it's about?" I asked.

No, she couldn't tell me, but she thought it was just some administrative formality. She suggested that I get excused from gym class in order to answer the summons early the next morning.

As I left the sun-filled office, I was blinded by the light reflecting off the glass covering a huge photograph of Hitler hanging on the wall. I planned to take the only official document I had, my Hitler Youth membership card, to the courthouse, hoping that Solomon's enormous lie wouldn't fall apart there. Actually, I was sure they were finally going to give me a German Reich identity card. And for that I was going to thank them with a particularly snappy Hitler salute.

I went back to class and then to work. That night, in spite of everything, I slept like a log. I was exhausted because Gerhard and I had stayed up late studying.

The next morning I headed for the court office that had sent the summons. I knew the way and so I walked at a leisurely pace. My classmates and I had often taken this same route to a nearby movie theater to watch films made by the Reich Film Production Center. There was a large pastry shop a few houses down from the courthouse. I had seen a sign on the shop's door. In clear black letters it read "No dogs or Jews allowed." For that very reason I went in whenever I passed by to purchase some cake or pastry. It pleased me to look the smiling saleswoman in the eye and hear her thank me obsequiously. But this was no time for Black Forest cherry cake.

The courthouse was a majestic structure that looked like an old royal palace. With my heart pounding, I went inside. An arrow pointed to the appropriate office; I went up to a rk, handed him my summons, and waited for his reaction. .ease sit down," he said politely and began to rummage ·ough a stack of papers. "Ah yes," he said, "this concerns getting a legal guardian for you." I was in seventh heaven. The threatening storm had passed, and unbounded joy spread through me.

I was asked to identify myself, and the clerk gave me some forms to fill out. Then I signed a formal document dealing with the appointment of a legal guardian. And who was it the legal authorities of Greater Germany had selected to be my guardian? None other than the former Waffen-SS officer, Home Leader Karl R., my immediate superior in the Hitler Youth. Here was another opportunity to break out the cognac and to drink a toast with him in honor of this touching turn of events. This was truly an extraordinary paradox, a unique anecdote in the history of the Third Reich. An SS officer was—unknowingly, of course—taking a Jewish child under his wing, in effect legally becoming his father.

I signed the document under the cold inquisitorial eye of the clerk. A silly notion struck me: In their eagerness and good will, would they one day marry me off to a blue-eyed girl with blond braids? Feeling on top of the world, I said good-bye to the clerk, and with a jaunty step and whistling a merry tune I hurried back to inform the home leader, my guardian, of his new role and to tell him how pleased I was about this new bond between us.

Once again, a "minor" danger had passed me by. I was overjoyed.

I ran along the paved path to Home 7. It would be empty at this hour. But unfortunately the home leader wasn't in his office. So I put on my work clothes to join my classmates in the workshop. Telling Karl the news would have to wait, and so would my plan to thank him.

When I walked into the workshop, some of the fellows looked up curiously and questioningly. I explained that everything was all right, it had only been some formality. I went to my work station and took up where I had left off the day before.

In the Strength-through-Joy [KdF] town of Wolfsburg they had been working full blast ever since 1940 on the design and production of the Volkswagen amphibious car, a vehicle that somewhat resembled the American Jeep. In our workshop, which, like the rest of the school and all its dormitories, belonged to the VW preproduction plant, we had to make special tools for the eventual mass production of this vehicle.

In the fall of 1942 an important event was scheduled to take place: the first trial run of this amphibian. We were among those invited to the celebration. A festively decorated bus took us to the VW factory in Wolfsburg. We all wore our best uniforms, carried swastika flags, and sang boisterously all the way there.

First we were shown the Volkswagen production line. The halls housing the punctiliously neat assembly lines were several hundred yards long. Paintings dealing with themes from German sagas and legends hung on the walls. The German designers, engineers, and technicians were easily recognized by the white smocks they wore. We also saw Dutch, Belgian, and French "guest workers" in these halls, as well as forced laborers, most of them from Poland. Naturally, they had to work even on this holiday. We generally looked down on anyone or anything that seemed strange or foreign, so we paid no attention to them. Besides, it was advisable not to talk to foreigners.

A colleague of Professor Porsche, the "father" of the Volkswagen, gave us a tour of the plant and explained the various manufacturing stages, starting with the assembly of the metal parts and concluding with the painting and finishing. At the very end of the incredibly long production line stood one of the vehicles, awaiting its trial run.

The Nazis considered this Volkswagen plant a model factory. It was financed in part through a unique savings campaign. The campaign slogan promised every German a KdF Volkswagen: "Save 5 Reichmarks every week if you want to drive your own car." However, when the campaign ended, none of the conscientious savers was rewarded with a car. The savings drive had less to do with passenger cars than with the financing of military equipment such as the amphibious vehicle, which in the end turned out to be a dud. But at the time, we cheered it as a sensational achievement.

Finally, after an ample midday meal, it was time to go to the proving grounds. We stood near the front row of spectators, looking at a steep downward slope that led to an artificial lake. People all around me were very excited as though this contraption would decide the outcome of the war and could lead to final victory.

Everyone was in a festive mood. We felt we really had had a share in this project. After all, hadn't we made the top-quality precision parts and hadn't we managed to finish them with amazing speed even before the deadline? These parts had been used in the chassis of the new vehicle. We were told its wheels would also "roll for victory." Suddenly, the order "Silence" was given. The important moment had arrived.

We heard motor noises, and then the amphibious car appeared at the top of the man-made hill. At first glance it looked just like an ordinary cross-country vehicle. But then it roared down the slope. The spectators held their breath in suspense until the car hit the water at the bottom of the slope with a huge splash. At that instant a kind of ship's propeller at the rear of the vehicle was switched on, and instead of sinking, the car actually floated! Everyone was entranced. Even I got carried away, joining in the stormy, exuberant applause.

And so the trial run was a success, "the fatherland was saved." But, as we know, even the invention of this amphibious vehicle couldn't prevent Germany's defeat.

We returned to Brunswick, overjoyed at the successful test run. The Hitler Youth homes, the classrooms, and the workshops were full of enthusiastic young people, now driven to even greater efforts and achievements.

We studied harder, and at the plant we worked with even greater dedication, drilling, screwing, and greasing the little wheels that were all part of Hitler's gigantic war machine. Later on, his "retaliatory" weapon, the V-1 rocket, was built in Wolfsburg too.

Meanwhile, daily life was disrupted and the morale of the population was undermined by the unremitting Allied air raids on cities and industrial centers. Victory seemed less certain. Blue-eyed Germans were beginning to see what was really happening, and they trembled as the blood hemorrhaged from their wounds.

One day our classes ended abruptly. We were ordered to go to the school auditorium to listen to a speech by the Minister of Propaganda, Joseph Goebbels. The speech was being broadcast direct from a mass meeting in the Berlin Sports Palace. Before Goebbels came on, an announcer described some of those in attendance: In the first row were seriously wounded war veterans wearing their medals; many were crippled or still in plaster casts. Behind them sat members of the *Wehrmacht*, delegations from the brown-and-black-uniformed organizations, and finally a large group of ordinary citizens.

What would Goebbels say? Then we heard his agitated voice. He stoked the heated atmosphere by drumming into his audience that the "unlimited reserves of strength" of the German people had not yet been exhausted. He sharply denounced the British and American air attacks as barbaric,

An assembly at the Hitler Youth school, Brunswick, Christmas 1942.

saying the Allies "were in the service of the Jews." Then he raised the emotional pitch another notch: "I ask you, do you want total war?" As the howling and excited crowd roared "Yes!" the fabric covering the loudspeakers vibrated so wildly, it almost tore.

So there was to be total war. Any enemy airman whose plane crashed on German territory could be lynched on the spot; nobody would be punished for it. In numerous prior speeches the British had been represented as natural and potential allies of Aryan Germany. Since they also had Aryan blood, the British had been urged to join Germany so that together they could free the West from the danger of Jewish Bolshevism. But that didn't happen, and now the Germans swore to retaliate; they built V-1 rockets and sang a song called "Bombs over England."

One day, the Deputy *Bannführer,* an honored war veteran who wore a wooden hand prosthesis covered by a glove, stopped me in the hallway of one of the dormitories. He told me that the following Sunday the *Bannführer* planned to introduce me to all the students of *Bann* 468 at the weekly muster. But then he disappeared so quickly down the hall that he couldn't possibly have heard my answer.

At first this news sent me into another tailspin. From then until the muster began, I lived in constant fear, feeling a deadly horror at the thought of standing up there before hundreds of suspicious and fanatical young Nazis. What if they suddenly had doubts about my origins? That would have led to unfriendly questions and investigations. These fears caused me deep psychological wounds that have not healed to this day, and probably never will.

The night before, I had a dream. I was standing before a troop of Nazis, all in dress uniforms, their hair neatly combed. Their penetrating stares pierced the protective shield behind which I was hiding. We were waiting for the arrival of the *Bannführer,* and it was taking forever. Finally, he walked in and casually said to the assembled Hitler Youths, "Look at this young Jew standing before you." The worst that could have happened happened: Screaming wildly, they pounced on me with unbridled frenzy, tore me limb from limb, and impaled my head on a flagpole.

I am still haunted by this dream; over the years it has hardly changed at all. The instant my head is impaled on the flagpole, I'm ripped out of my sleep, bathed in sweat and fighting for air. I continue to feel dazed while the fog gradually lifts; but once fully awake, I realize with happy relief that I'm still alive.

The actual muster turned out to be quite different. Despite my gruesome premonitions, it went surprisingly well. After the usual commands: "Company, halt! At ease! Attention! Eyes front!" *Bannführer* Mordhorst took over; he read the order of the day, which, in my bewilderment, I neither heard nor understood.

With my class at the Hitler Youth school (*Bann* 468), Brunswick, 1943. I'm third from the right in the next-to-last row.

Then he turned to me. I had been assigned to *Bann* 468 and had already started classes in the school, he said. The *Wehrmacht*, in which I had served on the eastern front in the 12th Panzer Division, had requested that this be arranged. He would now read the declaration the army had sent, which bore the signature of Lieutenant Colonel Becker. While he was reading, he emphasized words like "good conduct, courage, and exemplary behavior." To my relief I noticed that the same eyes I had been so afraid of were now looking at me with admiration, full of respect. *Bannführer* Mordhorst concluded solemnly, "As a token of our recognition of his service to the fatherland, the leadership of *Bann* 468 has resolved to award the rank of *Scharführer* to Hitler Youth Member Josef Perjell."

One of the reasons the other students admired me was that young Germans were all terribly eager to go to the front and to participate actively in the fighting. Whenever one of them reached draft age and his induction notice arrived, the news spread like wildfire through the school, and everyone came running to congratulate him and share in his joy. At the same time you could sense their envy: here was someone who was permitted to fight for his Führer and his *Volk*.

And now, at the Sunday muster, it was being announced in public that a seventeen-year-old newcomer had already participated in this "glorious" war, had served in a Panzer unit, had driven through Russia in an armored patrol car, and had done all this with bravery and courage.

With one fell swoop all the barriers came down. I was no longer an outsider trying to fit into an already existing community. I was accepted as a member, granted the same rights, and accorded the same respect.

Comfortable in my new position and breathing more freely, I felt my self-confidence growing.

5

LENI

The goals of National Socialism were preached continually at the school, and it was hammered into us that we represented the future elite of a new order. Some high-ranking Lower Saxony district party members, including the *Gauleiter* [Nazi party district leader], must have had these goals in mind when they arrived for an official visit. Our *Bannführer* walked over to greet them with long quick strides, clicked his heels, and smartly raised his arm. We did likewise. The *Gauleiter* turned around, faced us, and answered with a clipped *"Heil Hitler!"* Then he delivered a speech in which he told about his recent visit to the Führer's bunker, the Wolf's Lair. Hitler was running the military campaign from there, and the *Gauleiter* had come to our school, he said, to tell us about the Führer's imperturbability, his confidence and steadfastness. He wanted us to know that the Führer was Germany's best guarantee for final victory. As for the future, he said, "After victory, we shall rule the entire world, and we will need a hundred thousand leaders." Pointing at us, he predicted, "You will be those leaders!" There was absolute silence in the swastika-decorated hall. You could almost hear youthful chests swelling with a craving for greatness and glory, each youth enchanted by the idea of being a leader. And even Jupp mumbled to himself, "Did you hear that, Shloimele? Some day even you may become a little führer. . . ."

Toward the end of 1942, when the German victories had reached their apex and the eastern campaign was viewed as victorious, none of us had any doubts about the Third Reich. Even Jupp believed in it. One victory followed another, and the deluge of propaganda allowed no skepticism to develop. It was difficult for young people not to be impressed by the bright future they had been promised awaited them.

Occasionally I wondered how I would fit into this picture of a Germany that would rule the whole world. I got goose bumps thinking of the possibility that I too would get a fair share of glory, as the party people had said. But, as in the past, I was able to calm down. I counted on my ability to adapt in all situations, including a future German Reich that would rise out of the rubble of a "weak, demoralized Europe."

Whatever my role might turn out to be, I was certain of one thing: Jupp would never forget his primary commandment—to protect Solomon. The spark of Solomon's Jewish origins would continue to glow, never to be extinguished.

The life of Hitler Youth Jupp followed its prescribed course. I was glad that Karl R., who was more than just a home leader to me, had been named my guardian by the court. I developed a kind of trust in him, because from the start he had been honest and helpful. This reassured me and made me feel more secure. When he returned to his office, I went to thank him. We had a drink and we talked. Of course, he didn't know my background, but in spite of that we discovered a level on which we got along well and understood each other. But he could never have been a father-substitute for me. What an idea! At this very hour, my real and beloved father may have been perishing in the Lodz ghetto, victim of the inhuman and ultimately murderous Nazi decrees. I kept thinking, Dear God, won't you give me back my parents?

I often withdrew from the other students; I just wanted to be by myself. Therefore I only rarely went into town with them. Like the other fellows, I wanted to meet girls, but I was afraid to. All encounters that might have roused the curiosity of strangers had to be avoided. But by pure chance Ernst M., the "other" ethnic German, who came from the Ukraine—he was a few years older and only resided at the school, working outside—introduced me to a pretty BDM girl named Leni Latsch. I liked her right away. She aroused feelings I had to control and suppress. To tell the truth, I burned with desire for her from the moment we met. Leni had a great sense of humor. We complemented each other— she was happy and gregarious; I was serious and a loner.

We became friends, and our friendship turned into love.

I wanted to disclose my secret to Leni, but I didn't. This psychological tension of forbidden and therefore unfulfilled love made me increasingly sensitive. Then I found an outlet—I started to write poems.

One evening, alone in my room with the door locked, I composed several yearning, heartrending verses to my mother. I had never had poetic talent, but the simplest words sufficed to express my overwhelming suffering. I was a boy longing for a mother he had been forced to leave behind. And I could not mention or hint at any of this to my other love, Leni, who obeyed the laws and supported the goals of the Nazis. I felt drawn to her and she to me, and yet she knew neither who I was nor the tragic inner conflict I endured.

When the poem was finished, I read it to her while we were taking a romantic walk through the green fields outside

Leni.

the city. Naturally, I didn't tell her the real reason I was separated from my mother. We sat down with our backs to a thickly overgrown embankment, and I carefully pulled the poem out of my pocket and began reading:

Mother—
Even now I see you before me
Full of motherly love and devotion.
So let me greet you from afar.
May fate bring much happiness into your life.

My heart calls to you,
I love you so much.
Despite the distance that lies between us
Your heart is at the center of my being!
Can you feel my heart beating,
Can you see my tears flowing,
And how yearning consumes my soul
Because you are not here with me?
Can you hear my voice calling?
It calls to you, "Oh, Mother, Mother!"
And will not let me rest.
Do you see me swimming toward you, filled with yearn-
    ing?
For my one and only dream is always you.
Do you see me often weeping,
How my heart dissolves with love?
'Tis dreadful that fate
Has swept us apart.
Only one thing I long to know,
When shall we see each other again?
Will the hour of happiness strike for us once more?
Will destiny e'er bring me to your side?
Oh, I could walk a thousand miles
O'er land and across water, mountains, and valleys,
Through the icy cold and under the broiling sun,
If only to see you again, always!

Mutter —
Auch jetzt seh' ich Dich vor meinen Augen
So voller Mutterliebe und Herzenstreue
Drum sei gegrüßt aus weiter Ferne
Damit Dir das Schicksal viel Glück ins weitere Leben streue.
Mein Herz ruft ja so nach Dir,
Denn es hat Dich doch so gern,

Trotz der Ferne zwischen uns
Ist Dein Herz meines Herzens Kern!
Fühlst Du wie mein Herz so klopft,
Und die Träne aus dem Auge tropft,
Wie das Heimweh meine Seele frißt,
Nur weil Du bei mir nicht bist.
Hörst Du meine rufende Stimme?
Sie ruft nur— "Mutter, Mutter"—
Und läßt mir keine Ruh.
Merkst Du wie ich voll Sehnsucht zu Dir schwimme,
Denn mein einziger Traum bist nur noch Du.
Siehst Du wie ich des öfters weine,
Wie mein Herz aus Liebe nach Dir zergeht,
Furchtbar, daß gerade uns beide
Das Schicksal hat auseinandergeweht.
Und dieses möchte ich noch wissen,
Wann wir uns wiedersehen müssen,
Ob die Stunde des Glückes auch für uns mal wieder schlägt
Und das Schicksal mich zu Dir hinüberträgt!
Ich könnte tausende Kilometer gehen,
Durch Wasser, Land, Berg und Tal,
Bei eisgem Frost und heißem Sonnenstrahl,
Nur um Dich für immer wiederzusehen!

"A very moving poem," Leni said. For a while, she was silent, and then she stroked my hair. "Now I realize that an orphan can long for his mother even though he has never seen her or known her."

"Oh, Leni," I said, "a man always carries his mother within him. Didn't she give him life, even ordering him to live?" I was thinking of my mother's words the day she said farewell to me. . . .

Leni didn't know the reason for the upsurge of my emotion. I myself never told her anything about my mother's fate. But things would be different when it came to Leni's mother, a gentle, kind-hearted woman.

One day when I went to visit Leni, her mother opened the door and told me her daughter was not at home. I was about to leave and come back later, but she asked me to come inside; she wanted to talk to me, or so I assumed. Her tone of voice and her expression indicated this wasn't some casual invitation. She seemed to have something serious on her mind. Offering me a large antique easy chair, she sat down on the couch and gave me a perfunctory smile. I responded with a nervous laugh. Twilight made the prevailing mood of uncertainty even more oppressive. For several long minutes not a word was spoken. Then she said, "Tell me, Jupp, are you really German?"

Up to then, when confronted by unexpected questions, I had always had enough imagination to invent an appropriate lie. But now something strange was happening to me: Was it a mysterious feeling of trust? A sudden need to confess the precious secret that was consuming me? Momentary befuddlement? Was it faith that my lucky star wouldn't desert me this time either? I cannot explain it. At this decisive moment everything seemed to have come together to make me waver, to shake my rocklike determination, to move me to reveal my innermost secret. "No, Mrs. Latsch," I heard myself whisper, "I am not German; I'm Jewish."

I had answered her without feeling any inner conflict. But as soon as I said the words, I was shattered by what I had done. I knew I was still alive and breathing because I felt my body shaking and my knees trembling. Dazed by my own confession, I mumbled, "Please don't report me to the Gestapo."

Leni's mother got up and bent over me. She kissed my forehead, calmed me down, and promised not to reveal my secret to anyone. One single moment of human weakness, this breakdown of my marvelous defense and survival instincts, could have cost me my life. But once again I was miraculously protected. I felt that I had met a noble woman, a stranger who would understand. After getting a court-appointed father, I had found a mother for my emotional needs. . . .

This new relationship expressed itself through small kindnesses: darned socks or a piece of homemade cake. In return, I trusted her completely, convinced that she would never turn me in. On the contrary, she made me swear, no matter what, never to reveal my secret to her daughter. In this respect, not even Leni's own mother was sure of her daughter. "Children today are so different," was her only comment.

Having made my unanticipated, startling, and dangerous revelation, I asked her the inevitable question: Why had she become interested in my origins? It turned out that this knowing and sensitive woman had detected something odd about several of the things I had said. Twice, she pointed out, I became unintentionally tangled in the little lies I told about my family. Once I had said I was all alone in the world; another time I had said my grandparents were living in East Prussia. I no longer remembered why I had invented these details or when and where I had referred to them. But the truth far exceeded anything she had imagined about me. She had suspected that I wasn't German. But that I was Jewish!—she said she would never have dreamt that.

If all Germans had behaved like Heinz Kelzenberg and Maria Latsch, Eichmann and company would have been only miserable figures in the margins of history.

My confession to Mrs. Latsch brought me enormous relief, and I felt less alone and abandoned.

Not until after the war did I tell Leni the truth. She reacted in her own wry way. "Oh dear, I was guilty of Rassenschande *[racial disgrace]!" she said.*

Once she realized that I had been thinking of my mother in the Lodz ghetto when I first read her my poem, she was deeply moved. I also saw that her entire BDM system of racial theories came tumbling down when it dawned on her that she had spent considerable time with a Jew who respected her and who was closer to her than the Aryan friends who shared her political beliefs.

While I was in Brunswick, I frequently felt the urge to visit my former hometown, Peine. But since I didn't want to take any unnecessary risks, I resisted this longing. After all, it was only seven years ago that I had left Peine; someone there might easily recognize me as Solly, the little Jewish boy. In spite of this, one Sunday morning I gave in to a foolish recklessness; some devil must have been goading me. Once again I found myself at the Peine train station. When we were little, my playmates and I had often come down here. We used to stand on a wooden bridge that spanned the tracks and wait for the next train. When it arrived, clouds of smoke and steam would envelop us, hiding us from one another. Now I stood on that same bridge, but this time I didn't hear the happy laughter of my little friends. Instead I felt the miserable loneliness of the illegal and the persecuted.

Of course, it would never do to be recognized. I just wanted to take a nostalgic look at the scenes of my happy childhood, to immerse myself in the memories of my boyhood home and the kindergarten and school I had attended, now that I had neither a home nor any real friends. Then I would quickly leave again. I had left Peine an innocent lamb and returned like a sheep hunted by wolves. True, this particular sheep had learned to change its clothing so as to resemble the other wild beasts — it was the only way to escape the executioners. But what if the executioners were to get wind of something and get wise to these tricks? . . . Well, contrary to their racial theories, I had already determined that no particular odor clung to Solomon. So, let them sniff.

For quite a while, I gazed at the landscape from atop the wooden bridge, its planks worn down from the tramping of many hobnailed boots. I stood there and thought of another bridge, the metaphorical bridge of delusional ideas across which they had chased me into exile. But my bridge had ultimately been burned behind me. Would it some day again extend over the tracks for me? Some day would I stand here as Solly Perel, a free man?

I straightened my black-and-brown uniform, adjusted my black tie and the swastika armband, and slowly started to walk down the steps to the sidewalk. So as not to draw any curious looks from passersby, I turned my face toward the shop windows, and there I saw a familiar facade that brought me pain and sorrow. There was a time, eons ago, when this shop had belonged to my parents. Now it was a photographer's studio. No longer was my father's stock of shoes on display; instead, framed photographs of *Wehrmacht* soldiers, their arms encircling wife and child, stood on the shelves. At the entrance to the store I remembered moments from a happy childhood, when I would boisterously run in and ask for a coin to buy an ice cream cone. If the store was full of customers, my father would reprimand me, and I would wait impatiently until he had time for me. Eventually the smile and the coin he gave me would make everything all right again.

But I also remembered a less happy incident. In the store one day my father had asked me to take some money to my mother at home. She was going to use it to pay for a coal delivery for our furnace. That particular day happened to be my best friend Hans Meiners' birthday. So I naively decided to show my affection for him by getting him a present. At Spinzig's in the market square, the biggest toy store in town, I bought a model of a famous sailboat for five marks. At first Mrs. Spinzig refused to take her eight-year-old customer seriously and suggested I come back with my mother. But I stubbornly managed to persuade her to sell me the boat model. Proudly I carried the beautiful birthday present to Hans' house, and wishing him a happy birthday, I handed it to him. His mother frowned. Very pleased with myself, I skipped home and gave my mother the rest of the money. Without mentioning my purchase, I turned to other things as though nothing had happened.

But then Mrs. Meiners appeared in our apartment, whispering in painful embarrassment in my mother's ear. I sensed something was wrong. Wearing a severe expression, my mother asked me to explain. I blushed and stammered that Mrs. Meiners' story was true. Mama put on her coat, and the three of us went over to the Meiners' apartment. There in the living room stood the wonderful birthday present. I was ordered to take it back. At the toy store, Mrs. Spinzig shook her head, probably thinking, I knew it, I knew it. . . . Shamefaced, I carefully put the sailboat on the counter and, feeling rather despondent, left it there. But this painful business was not yet finished. When my father came home from the store at the end of the day and heard what I had done, he gave me an unforgettable spanking.

Now these memories engulfed me. I thought of my parents; I thought of Lodz. I wished I were there with them.

Standing in front of the shop windows that had once belonged to us, I also recalled an evening in 1933 at the dawn of the "Thousand-Year Reich." SA Storm Troopers had smeared our windows with long streaky letters: "Don't buy from Jews!" After that, the shop stayed closed. Little by little we transferred the stock to our apartment. There were still some brave and loyal customers who wanted to buy their shoes and shoelaces from us, and after dark they would furtively stop by.

Now, nine years had passed, years of suffering and tragedy. And here I stood, bewildered, shaken, and disoriented, dreaming of the past, disillusioned with the world.

"Wake up, come to your senses, think of the present!" an inner voice warned me. I roused myself. The stores were all closed. Most people were attending Sunday church services. Long ago, I used to sneak into a church to hear the organ play and to listen to the choir sing chorales. Now I walked over to the market square, where the quiet atmosphere of a Sunday morning prevailed. Spinzig's store windows were overflowing with toys, but my model sailboat was not among them. When I turned left toward my former school, I was overcome with emotion. The gate and the classrooms were open, even on Sundays. I looked around, and since I didn't see anyone, I went inside. The familiar smell of floor wax and the sight of the school desks and their inkwells made me feel nostalgic. I sat down in my old seat where I had listened to my teacher, Mr. Philipps, tell his unforgettable stories about wonderful journeys to enchanted stars. Under his direction, we used to recite the alphabet in the same repetitive singsong over and over.

But it was here, in this school, where a dance of death and my flight from the angel of death had begun. One day, while sitting in class, I was ordered to go to the school principal's office. He gave me a letter for my parents and told me to pack up my things and go home. Just like that. "Take your school bag and get out." I left sobbing, too young to know why I had been expelled.

The storm began that day. Nothing was certain any more—I had no future, only a present full of ordeals and emotional shocks. I had become a hunted refugee in perpetual flight.

Sitting on one of the little school benches, I tried to forget this part of my past, tried once more to be the boy I used to be. It didn't work; those days were gone, irretrievably and forever.

Given my agitated state, I really should have headed back to Brunswick immediately, but first I wanted to take a look at the house at 1 Am Damm, where I was born and where I had lived. It was just a few minutes' walk from the school. I knew every paving stone and every corner. At this spot I was once knocked down by someone riding a bicycle but, like a big boy, had picked myself up and had gone on playing. And over there, next to the wall of that house, we used to play marbles. . . .

I walked along, deep in thought. Now I was standing across the street from our house. A former neighbor, Mr. Nachtway, was looking out of his window. I almost said hello to him but, afraid he would recognize me, I turned away. The old man had known me well. I used to sit on his lap while he told exciting children's stories. And now I couldn't even say hello to him.

A young woman appeared at one of the windows of our former apartment. She couldn't possibly know that the uniformed Hitler Youth standing on the other side of the street had once lived happily in those very rooms. I was born there, I had laughed and cried there, and I had been sick and gotten well again in that house. Now I was barred from going in. The large, greenish-colored building where the Meiners family lived adjoined our red brick house, and together they formed the street corner. I couldn't set foot in that house either, even though I used to spend most of my time with the children who lived there. The Meiners' beer tavern and a meeting hall called the Luisenhof were in the right wing of the building. Now a huge sign proclaimed "German Labor Front—Peine Chapter."

In the spacious inner courtyard of the tavern building there used to be a pigsty, a barn, and a public urinal. No need to describe the mixture of odors emanating from them. Other memories crowded in: When I was still living here, I was always afraid of the drunkards who, raucously singing old popular songs, would come out to urinate after their beer drinking. Some would talk to themselves and curse every-

A motorcycle license photo showing me at age eighteen, 1943.

thing that crossed their paths. I was usually on hand when a pig was about to be slaughtered. I was fascinated by the squeals of the pig and admired the skillful hands that did the killing. The Meiners children—Clara, Thea, and Hans—and I used to secretly play "father, mother, and child" among the bales of hay in the barn.

The local Communists and Social Democrats held their meetings in the Luisenhof. I'd listen to their passionate speeches without having the slightest idea of what they were talking about. I understood only that after the failure of their alliance against National Socialism, a fight had erupted between them. Their quarrel proved the old adage "When there are three, and two are fighting, the third is happy." Most of the time the meetings did not end peacefully. Gangs of SA men accompanied by Hitler Youths often would storm into the hall. Sometimes knives and daggers flashed, and several of the participants were wounded. Emil, the butcher's apprentice, who also worked as a waiter in the beer hall and who was one of my brother's best friends, was beaten to death during one of these brawls. The police were usually very slow to take a hand, and when they finally did, they arrested the victims of the attacks.

I had not intended to visit the Meiners' tavern. From the outset, such recklessness seemed tantamount to suicide. But somehow, an irresistible force had drawn me there, and I found myself sitting at one of the little square tables.

In the dense smoke that hung over the room, customers were slurping foaming beer from giant mugs. The Meiners were eating lunch at their customary table. Mrs. Meiners, as fat as ever, hadn't changed; neither had her husband's bald pate. The daughters had turned into attractive young women. My boyhood friend Hans wasn't with them, and I assumed he had already been drafted. Suddenly I shuddered; I should have left instantly, but I sat there as though glued to my seat, my legs like lead. All my alarm mechanisms had failed; my senses, which were usually so keen, were not functioning. How else could I have gotten myself into such a predicament? The Meiners used to have liberal, almost leftist, political viewpoints. Presumably they had stuck to their convictions, but how could one know to what degree they— like so many others—had been influenced by Nazi propaganda? This forbidden encounter of the past and present could end in catastrophe for me. Born in Peine; done for in Peine? I bitterly regretted my reckless behavior; I had contravened my mother's command to fight for my life. But now there was no going back.

Clara was the first to notice the new customer. She put down her knife and fork, wiped her hands, and rose from her chair to take my order. The die was cast.

With the polite, impersonal smile of a waitress, she approached my table. Pulling myself together with all my might, I tried to act calm so as not to raise her suspicions. And, above all, I didn't want to make eye contact with her. Would she have the nerve to ask me whether I was Solly? Or would she be so unsure that she'd rather not say anything? After all, the young man sitting at the table was a model Hitler Youth, a *Scharführer* in all his glory. Even if I did resemble Solly, she'd say to herself, That isn't possible; it's unthinkable!

I ordered a mixed beer, half dark, half light. There's no doubt that at that instant I was out of my mind, for I raised my head and looked straight at her. She looked back at me searchingly. A wave of fear surged through me, and I decided that if she recognized me, I would adamantly deny everything. But then, with disinterest, she looked away again, took my order, and went on with her work. Apparently, it hadn't even occurred to her to ask me questions. I became somewhat calmer as I realized she was behaving naturally and wasn't intentionally ignoring me. She simply hadn't recognized me. I paid and hastily emptied my mug. Clara returned to the family table, and I quietly slipped away. On the way to the train station I did not look back, not even once. I walked quickly because I had the feeling that someone was following me and could bar my way at any moment. I boarded the first train to Brunswick.

When I recently met Clara Meiners Frieling, she did not remember any of this. She said that quite a few Hitler Youths were regular customers at the tavern, and she could not remember any special incident.

Of course, I didn't tell Gerhard about my secret visit to Peine. I vowed never to go back to that forbidden city, except as a free man returning to a free city.

And yet a powerful and imperative need kept driving me toward all things that reminded me of home.

I developed a warm relationship with Miss Köchy, and we spent some pleasant times together. Occasionally she invited me to accompany her to concerts or to the opera in the Brunswick civic theater. Those evenings were an enriching cultural experience for me. But there was one longing I couldn't suppress: the yearning to be in a family setting, safe and secure, no matter how briefly. My childhood and youth had been spent in an orphanage, in the trenches and bunkers, and in the houses of strangers. I longed for a warm, loving atmosphere, for the aroma of a cake baking in our old oven. . . . I envied my classmates who had families. Whenever I was invited to go home with one of the other students, I would eagerly look around me, intent on soaking up the details of normal family life. And for that reason I was delighted when Miss Köchy invited me to her cozy apartment. I had almost forgotten the feel of places like hers, and I liked being there. It was consoling to imagine my parents there with me, and it stilled my painful yearning. For my hostess this was just a normal courtesy call. Not so for me. After that, I often dropped in on Miss Köchy, and I will never forget those visits.

In the summer of 1943 Miss Köchy's family arranged for me to spend my vacation with their close relatives in Thale, a small town in the Harz Mountains, a region of extraordinary beauty. I took solitary walks through the surrounding area, feeling free and happy. It was here that the poet and philosopher Goethe wrote a portion of his famous *Faust* while sitting on a boulder near a crystal clear spring, surrounded by the bright green mountains. From the top of a hill across the way,

On a trip to a cavern near Harz, summer 1943. On this occasion, I was the guest of one of my officers. I am between the two women in the center.

I thought I could make out the clearing where Goethe's witches danced, and where at the stroke of midnight they were supposed to have set off on their satanic ride.

Sitting on Goethe's rock, surrounded by mystery, I gave in to daydreams of my boyhood home: The pain of longing for my parents stung like a thousand needles. I tore a page from my notebook and wrote a personal, yearning manifesto—a confession and an accusation against the world and its Creator. While I was still struggling to articulate my thoughts, a young couple came by. They spoke French and were probably *Fremdarbeiter*, the foreign workers who were identifiable by an emblem they had to wear on their clothes. They took off their clothes behind some dense shrubbery and jumped into the stream. The mountains echoed with their joyful shouts, as though they wanted to say, "Don't despair! The future belongs to us, belongs to you. . . ."

And at that moment, in that place, I wrote my manifesto: "I, Solomon Solly Perel, a Jew, son of Rebecca and Azriel, the younger brother of Isaac, David, and Bertha, leave this statement for the world. Lord, God who are in heaven, who created the earth and mankind, how can you let an innocent child be condemned to the loneliness and torment of such gruesome persecution? I no longer have the strength to endure it. I beg you, give me back my home, my father and my mother. I pray that the day may soon arrive when we are reunited and free. Amen." I neatly folded the piece of paper and, with a silent prayer, solemnly put it into a tin box I had found. Then, with tears running down my cheeks, I buried the box deep in a crack in the boulder on which I had been sitting.

6

OTTO

I was very interested in chess and spent my free evenings playing with a fellow student, Otto Zagglauer. I had taught him the basics of the game, and he became a devoted player and was happy to be my regular partner. One day, as we were engrossed in our moves, he asked me, "Who taught you to play so well?"

"Some former friends," I said sadly, suddenly transported by a flood of memories to another time and place.

These friends were Jerzyk Rappoport and Jakob Lublinski. We were a threesome in our class in Lodz: Jakob, Jerzyk, and Salek, the Polish name for Solly. I was twelve, maybe thirteen years old. The three of us studied and played together, shared the same emotions, and gradually discovered the adult world. There were minor differences of opinion, but they weren't serious. I joined the Zionist Gordonia Club, whereas my friends were enthusiastic members of the *Bund*. The *Bund* was an anti-Zionist, Jewish political party of the extreme left. But that didn't keep me from going to their club once in a while to read the Yiddish papers and to listen to lectures. Later I also joined the *Bund*, and that's where my two friends initiated me into the intricacies of chess. We would sit there for hours, bent over a chessboard.

When war broke out, we lost touch with one another. Jerzyk and Jakob stayed in Lodz, and I went east with my brother Isaac.

After the war I found out that Jerzyk had remained true to his convictions. During the war he was the leader of the Politburo of the Communist party in the Lodz ghetto. His courageous deeds gave hope and strength to many of the people there. Jerzyk's short life ended tragically. He managed to survive all the suffering and misery of the war and was liberated by soldiers of the Red Army. After that, he fell passionately and deeply in love with a Jewish girl who did not return his affections and married someone else. He could not cope with this loss; his instinct for survival and the enormous strength that had made it possible for him to endure the Shoah *now deserted him, and he committed suicide.*

I did see Jakob again. One day, while I was still in the Grodno orphanage, we were told there would be a concert by amateur musicians from a high school in Minsk. When the members of the orchestra arrived, I spotted Jakob among them.

We threw our arms around each other. I didn't leave his side until the concert started, and later we talked until dawn, laughing and shedding tears of joy and sorrow. After this touching reunion I never saw Jakob again.

It was painful to remember all this. I couldn't very well tell my chess partner Otto about any of it. But I must say I felt great whenever I could checkmate him. For being his teacher and partner, he gave me a valuable chess set that he brought from home after one of our vacations. I still use it today.

One day Otto invited me to see a film with him, a comedy with the actor Heinz Rühmann. In those days films—corny melodramas with happy people living in secure comfort—usually had happy endings. This was so completely contrary to my personal circumstances that it unsettled me emotionally and intensified my sorrow instead of assuaging it. Nevertheless, I often went to the movies as a diversion and, of course, to see the weekly newsreel.

On the way to the theater we passed a large poster pasted on a kiosk. It showed a horrible-looking Jew loaded down with diamonds, with a repulsive face and a protruding belly. The caption read "The Jew Instigates and Prolongs Wars."

Otto's expression changed. His face flushed and his chin began to tremble. Looking a little ridiculous, he reached for his dagger and boasted, half in jest, half seriously, "If only I had one of these Jews here right now . . . !"

I didn't know whether to laugh or to object, so I didn't react at all. In spite of the anger boiling in me, I controlled myself. "Come on, otherwise we'll be late for the film," I said, and pulled him along. Again I was able to keep calm, but I couldn't get the poster out of my mind. This wasn't just a harmless message, but typical Nazi propaganda that turned the Jew into a scapegoat. Their hopes for a *Blitzkrieg* had failed; on the eastern front the army was stuck in the mud; and there were signs of discontent even on the home front. People were bitter over the suffering and the price countless victims were paying. In the midst of all this, Reich Propaganda Minister Joseph Goebbels asked the German people the inflammatory question, "Do you know who is responsible for this terrible situation? The Jews. They forced the war on us, and they want to prolong it so they can get rich."

My friend Otto couldn't have known that within a short time not many Jews would be left in Europe and that his own countrymen were getting rich from the diamonds, the gold teeth, the bones, and the hair of dead Jews. At the time I, Jupp, didn't have any inkling either. Even though we had been taught in class that the extermination of the Jews was necessary, we were not told how or when.

The film, which was quite enjoyable, made me temporarily forget the pain and the anger the poster had caused me.

Nearly all the people in the theater were women; most men had been drafted. Only a few old men and soldiers on furlough from the front were left at home, in addition to the *Fremdarbeiter*, the foreign workers.

Later on, Otto was to play a different role in my life. It may seem odd, but I gave in to the Jupp in me and saw him once after the war. That was in 1947, in Munich. I was living with my brother Isaac at the time, and some of his Jewish friends who had survived the concentration camps had gotten together at his house. When I told them that I had been a member of the Hitler Youth, they said, "You're making this up."

"I can prove it to you," I insisted, because suddenly I thought of Otto, who also lived in Munich. Actually I knew only his name and his birth date, but that was enough for the State Residents' Registration Office, and they gave me his address. I could hardly wait to see him. A streetcar and a bus brought me to his apartment house. The card under the doorbell said "Zagglauer Family."

His mother opened the door. "Come in," she said, "my son is at home."

I hadn't yet grown used to my changed situation, this priceless treasure called freedom. It was all so new. The Jupp in me was getting together with his old comrade, something that left Solly completely cold. When Otto walked into the room, we stood facing each other. He was obviously happy to see me, and I was beaming too. But at first it was Solly who spoke, eager to tell him about the triumph of life. How long had I waited for this chance, and now the moment of truth was at hand. "Otto, listen. I want to tell you a se-

cret. I'm not German; I'm 100 percent Jewish." Otto turned pale, and there was an embarrassing silence. The blood drained from his face, and he asked how I had managed to conceal all that. If he felt other emotions, he suppressed them.

After I told him my story, he looked at me, shaken, and said, "Yes, I'll admit the Nazis deceived us. The tragedy is that the people, especially the young people, allowed themselves to be so easily hoodwinked by their leaders' propaganda, that they firmly believed in the sincerity, the uprightness of their own country." His naïveté stunned me. I felt no sympathy for him. Still, we sat there for quite some time; there was so much to tell each other. And then I invited him to come with me to my brother's apartment the following Sunday. Understandably, he hesitated when I told him who would be there. In spite of that he agreed to join us.

Sunday I took him to Isaac's place. Mira had baked a traditional cheesecake for the occasion.

The same people who had doubted my story were there. Otto and I told them about our experiences as Hitler Youths in Brunswick. And with that their last remaining doubts about the truth of my story were laid to rest. In turn, Otto finally received confirmation that I was Jewish.

While we were in the HJ home, we were given one evening off every two weeks. Usually we'd go to a *Bierstube*, a tavern, to have a beer and a meal of mashed potatoes and vegetables, the only food you could get without ration coupons.

A pretty BDM girl who had many lovers, some of them members of our group, often joined us.

One day several of these fellows were summoned to undergo a medical examination. There was talk that the girl had caught the clap (gonorrhea) and had infected several of the guys.

It caused a tremendous stir in our citadel of "purity and honor." Outrageous! What a scandal!

With my Hitler Youth school comrades, Brunswick, 1943. I am in the
center in front.

I had never played around with this girl, but I was afraid
that all of those who had been seen with her might be ordered to take the physical examination. Under no circumstances could I let that happen to me. I was as tense as a bow-
string. But gradually fewer of these summonses arrived at the

house, and finally they stopped coming altogether. Evidently my name wasn't on their list. I started to breathe easier. Once again the days of worried waiting were over and the incubus of imminent detection and death had again been lifted.

It was December 1943, and the Christmas vacation was close at hand. One evening I was sitting in the reading room looking up background material for a discussion I was to have with some fourteen-year-olds who had just arrived. As *Scharführer* in charge of this group I was supposed to tell them about the importance of the German *Bauerntum* [peasantry] who proudly "kept the blood and race pure." I settled down to go through a big pile of literature on this subject. Having always been hungry for knowledge and in spite of the utter inappropriateness of the role I had to play, I cheerfully did my job and gave it my best. I played Jupp to the hilt. The boys in the group liked me and respected the "old veteran" who had fought with a Panzer division. It helped to be familiar with their thought processes; I knew their minds were already irretrievably befogged and manipulated, and I knew which way the wind was blowing here. So it was easy for me to compose lectures in the spirit of National Socialism.

That evening, as I was organizing my lecture, I overheard some of the students at the next table talking in subdued voices. I heard them say that they had already received their Christmas vacation permits as well as their train tickets. They were looking forward to seeing their families again soon. The phrase "at my parents' house" hit me more and more insistently. My dry lips wordlessly repeated, "at my parents' house," and a feeling of deep loneliness gnawed at me. I grabbed all the literature on the table and furiously put it back on the shelf. As though I'd been stung by a tarantula, I ran over to the office to see Miss Köchy. My inner voice protested angrily, "Jupp, all of these boys are going to spend their vacation with their parents; you're the only one who'll

be spending it alone. You've got nobody who's close to you."
Well, it was going to be different this time. I, Solly, had parents too, and the fact that they were imprisoned in the ghetto didn't change that. I had a right to them, just as any child would. Even if it costs you your life? I asked myself. In my excited state, the question seemed to be irrelevant. I didn't want to admit the danger I was about to put myself in. Waves of profound longing rolled over me, and I allowed them to carry me along.

I would go to the Lodz ghetto.

In the office Miss Köchy had her hands full with preparations for the numerous students' vacation trips. All students going away for the Christmas vacation needed to be provided not only with a permit but also food ration cards, pocket money, and round-trip train tickets. She and the personnel manager were looking through a stack of papers when I came bursting in. "I would like to go on vacation. Would you please make out the required travel documents for me," I said in a firm voice. They stared at me. After a while, the manager said, "Oh, and where would you like to go?"

"To Lodz."

"And why would you want to go to Litzmannstadt?" he wanted to know. The Nazi stickler insisted on the German name for Lodz.

"I want to settle some affairs," I explained, my voice a little uncertain.

His voice, on the other hand, became stern. "I will not grant this leave. We're responsible for your welfare and safety. And you'd be putting yourself unnecessarily in danger. However, I would be happy to have you celebrate Christmas Eve with me and my family."

I was crestfallen. It was starting to look as if I couldn't carry out my spur-of-the-moment decision. Miss Köchy noticed my disappointment, and she cut in and "explained" to her boss my puzzling desire to travel. She pointed out that the newspapers had recently been carrying reports dealing with new settlements in the conquered Polish territories; it was part of the Germanization plan. Thousands of ethnic Germans from the east would be moved there; among them might well be people from Grodno. And, she continued, *Scharführer* Josef was probably hoping to find people from his hometown who might be able to give him information about members of his family. She added that Josef was a very independent young man, that he had combat experience at the front, and that one could depend on him. I was touched by Miss Köchy's innocent assumptions and thanked her silently for her good will. She had no idea, of course, how close to the truth she had come! I really did intend to look up acquaintances and relatives: above all, I wanted to find my parents.

In 1985, when I returned to Brunswick, I went to visit Miss Köchy. She readily remembered my request back in 1943 and told me something that shocked me: my desire to go to Lodz had surprised several people at the boarding school and had given rise to some dangerous speculation about me.

I thanked the personnel manager for his friendly invitation to spend the Christmas holidays with him and his family. But I repeated my request to be allowed to go to Lodz. Miss Köchy backed me up, pointing out that she personally didn't see anything wrong with such a trip. Finally, the manager agreed to let me go.

"I'm very much obliged. Thank you," I said. "*Heil Hitler!*"

All sorts of questions raced through my mind: Where would this daring enterprise lead me? The dream of finding my parents belonged to another world, a totally different reality, but it was my most fervent wish that it come true. I faced a human adventure that held the possibility for good or evil, happiness or annihilation. Whatever might happen after that didn't matter.

Meanwhile, I prepared for my trip and obtained the required documents: an official vacation permit, a Hitler Youth membership card, a driver's license, food ration cards, and some pocket money. The HJ laundry sent over meticulously ironed brown uniform shirts. I carefully brushed my winter uniform, paying special attention to every badge, each insignia of rank, and every decoration.

This unusual undertaking was quite risky. I couldn't afford to make a single mistake. It was as if someone had written the script and I had to play my role persuasively down to the smallest detail. A long train trip was about to take me into another realm where two worlds, light-years apart, were in collision. I stood between them, stood in each of them, and thus in neither of them.

I knew what awaited me but didn't want to admit that I knew. Nor did I concede what might happen. Would I slip up, fall victim to an uncontrollable temptation, and perish? I naively thought that I would see my parents again, spend my school vacation with them, and then come back here. Why should it surprise any of my classmates that Hitler Youth Solomon should want to do what they were doing?

The half-formed dream, the despairing cry of a lonely child, became real the day I said good-bye to the other boys, who were also leaving on vacation. I tried hard not to let my emotions show. I wished them all a Merry Christmas and said I was looking forward to seeing them again soon. But would I be coming back? Would they ever see me again? I didn't know. But these questions really didn't bother me, didn't stand in the way of my plans.

Dressed in my uniform decorated with all my medals and insignia, I headed for the train station. The trip would be difficult. I had to be prepared for strict Gestapo and Kripo [Criminal Police] checks. These police organizations had the authority to arrest anyone, throw him into prison, and torture and murder him. Although the Gestapo was a political secret service and the Kripo was concerned with criminal infractions, there was no difference between them when it came to the "liquidation of hostile elements," such as Jews.

But knowing this did not intimidate me. I took the streetcar to the train station, and when the train arrived, I made myself comfortable in one of the compartments. The stationmaster gave the signal, and the train began to move.

7

To Lodz

I immersed myself in newspapers, reading all about the "strategic realignment of the eastern front." Actually, what official sources were euphemistically calling victory should have read "retreat." I looked up from my paper and watched plowed fields flying by. Again, I was assailed by doubts. An inner voice whispered, "Wake up; it doesn't make any sense to continue this trip! Go back to Brunswick. You're risking your life for something you'll never be able to bring off. Don't lose your perspective. Don't ruin everything!" I poked my head out of the train window, hoping the wind would blow away these gloomy premonitions. Then, to settle my nerves, I sat back and bit into a smoked-meat sandwich.

Contradictory thoughts kept flashing through my mind. The voice of misgiving became louder, trying to appeal to reason. But no power on earth could have gotten me to turn back. The train continued to chug eastward.

I slid back and forth in my seat. My eyes wandered from the landscape to my newspapers, but I could no longer concentrate on the printed words. I tried to sleep a little, but my knees were trembling with nervousness. The monotonous rattle of the train mingled with the subdued conversations of the other passengers and the occasional slamming of compartment doors. Outside the wind whistled. Suddenly I heard a commanding voice. "Have your papers ready for inspection!" The lights in the compartment were turned on, and Jupp came to attention. Josef Perjell from Northern Lower Saxony was ready for security control. The sliding door opened, and two stern-looking men walked in. They were wearing long black winter coats and broad-brimmed hats. Identifying themselves as police, they carefully examined the papers of the other passengers in the compartment, fixing everyone in turn with a cold stare. One man was asked to give the reason for his trip, another had to open his bag. Then it was my turn.

Without hesitating I handed over my travel permit and my Hitler Youth membership card. By my bearing I tried to show them that I understood the need for this security check. The two officers, who seemed to have long experience with the procedure, looked at me briefly, returned my papers, and saying, "Thank you, *Heil Hitler!*" they left, closing the door behind them.

I took a deep breath. Another obstacle had been overcome. Dangerous minutes had passed without incident. Had they discovered what a first-class prize I represented, they would have dragged me to their Gestapo cellar. The arrest of a Jew disguised as a Hitler Youth, what congratulatory pats on the back that would have brought them. . . .

We crossed the border. The names of the towns and the landscape showed that we were now in Poland, approaching Lodz.

Late at night, the train pulled into Kaliszki Station in Lodz. I had already decided not to go to a hotel, in order to avoid unnecessary risks. I didn't want to have anything to do

with a Polish hotel reception clerk who would ask me to fill
out a registration form. There wasn't anybody better than
those people at recognizing Jewish faces, actually "sniffing
them out." I preferred to renounce both comfort and danger
and spend the night in the train station, which teemed with
people both day and night. No one would notice if I
stretched out on one of the broad wooden benches in a corner of the waiting room.

By using a different bench every night I hoped to avoid
becoming conspicuous. I would take all possible precautions
not to fall into the hands of German secret police officers or
Polish informers who were always lurking about.

At least half of me was beyond reproach; I was wearing a
uniform, and I had genuine documents. But the other half
might easily arouse suspicions through his highly unusual
behavior.

I checked my suitcase in the baggage room, holding on
only to the essentials. Then I ambled through the station
that I had come to know well years before after getting to be
a "big boy." Kaliszki was a huge railroad junction; innumerable travelers streamed in and out at all hours. I wandered
around, remembering. I had often taken trains from this station in the days when the sun still shone for me.

A few weeks after my family and I had moved to Lodz
from Peine, a close relative on my father's side had invited
me to spend my vacation in Ciechocinek, one of the best-
known health resorts in Poland. I liked the town with its gardens of red and white flowers—the Polish national colors,
symbols of innocence and love. On the train to Ciechocinek,
I caused my relative some problems because I kept throwing
up. A wise old woman on the train suggested a remedy for
my nausea. She advised sitting in a seat that faced forward, in
the direction the train was going. That fixed it.

On the dangerous trip I had just completed, I also suffered from nausea, but for different reasons. . . .

I remembered other exciting vacations. At the end of the 1938 school year my parents sent me to Chelm and Zamosc to stay with cousins of my father. I was welcomed warmly. They called me Shloimele, the little *Yecke* [German Jew]. My hosts owned lumberyards outside the town in a singularly barren area. While I was with them I attended the magnificent wedding of their son. My room was adjacent to that of the young couple, and my bed stood along the wall that divided the two rooms. After the celebration, I was awakened late at night by unusual noises coming from the adjoining room. I quickly tiptoed over to the door and looked through the keyhole. I saw moving shadows and imagined all kinds of things. It was the first time that I found out about the physical aspect of love. The young couple hadn't noticed me. . . . But the experiences on this visit to Zamosc were not limited to a furtive peep through a keyhole. I was exposed to a Yiddish world I had not known before and that soon would be obliterated. We spent pleasant carefree days there; no one could have known what would soon be happening in a nearby town called Treblinka. Today I am deeply saddened and dismayed when I think of the tragic fate of the wedding guests, my relatives, and the young bride and groom. Sometimes when I talk about Treblinka, I see them again as they were then. It's heartbreaking to recall these dear people who will never come back from that death camp.

At the end of the 1939 school year, I brought home an outstanding report card from Konstadt elementary school in Lodz. My parents took me on vacation to a little Polish village named Kolumno. After that, I was happily looking forward to starting at the Jewish high school in Lodz.

But things turned out differently. The invasion of Poland by the *Wehrmacht* brought these plans and our lighthearted vacation days in the beautiful environs of Kolumno to an abrupt end. We couldn't take the train home because the railroad tracks had been destroyed by German bombs.

So we borrowed a horse-drawn cart from a Polish peasant and somehow made it back to Lodz. It was four months later that my parents ordered my brother and me to take flight.

And now, four years later, I had come back, in secret but with valid identification papers; a free man, but only in outward appearance.

At the railroad station, I was tormented by memories. I couldn't sleep and spent the seemingly endless hours among many other travelers who were waiting in the station. A few cups of ersatz coffee helped me to make it through the long, cold night. Excitedly, I looked forward to what would happen the next morning. My parents were living under this same sky, in this same city; yet they were as far away from me as if they were on a forbidden planet, beyond all borders—and all because of the madness perpetrated by the Nazi racists.

Before daybreak, after stretching my stiff and weary limbs, I went to the public toilets to wash and to check my appearance. Then I started out. Solomon-Jupp confidently walked down the stone stairs of the railroad station and over to the main streetcar terminal. There I looked for the trolley that would take me to the Lodz ghetto. My parents had sent me their address on a postcard they mailed to the orphanage in Grodno, and so I knew where they lived. On the first car of the trolley a sign read "For Germans Only." Without hesitating, I climbed aboard. After all, I was a *Reichsdeutscher* now, a genuine German. I hoped that I could become the person I really was as soon as I reached the vicinity of the ghetto. But who was I?

The departure signal, the ringing of the electric bell, brought me back to reality. My journey had begun. I was anxious to rediscover all the streets I had known, and as we approached the center of the city via Piotrkowska Street, the buildings looked increasingly familiar. We passed the Lodz branch of Gentleman, the store from which, shortly before it was plundered, my brother had rescued the collapsible umbrellas that financed our trip to the east. Once this flourishing city had been a lively commercial center. Artur Rubinstein was born here. Dzigan and Szumacher and other Jewish artists had flourished here. Now Lodz resembled a ghost town. Its Polish inhabitants, humiliated and treated like scum by the German occupation forces, skulked through the streets. Some of the shops and restaurants served only Germans. And I was riding in a car of the trolley that was off limits to Poles. . . .

Even in my necessarily compromised situation, it was hard to understand and to accept the servility and baseness of some of the Polish population. Antisemitic fascists and bootlickers threw themselves down in the dust before the new German masters from the west. They shamefully offered to collaborate with them, instead of closing ranks with their own countrymen who were fighting for a free Poland, for the freedom of mankind.

I almost missed my stop. It used to be called Freedom Square, and once it was a charming place bordered by beautiful public buildings decorated with statues and picturesque balconies. The Germans had renamed Lodz, calling it Litzmannstadt, and they also gave this square a different name. Several major streets started out from here. One of them, Nowomaiska Avenue, led to the ghetto. I walked the rest of the way and arrived at the corner of Polnotzna Street, a corner I still remembered well. Several houses had been torn down to create a border strip around the ghetto. It would make escape attempts more difficult. Before the war I used to visit relatives who lived at 6 Polnotzna Street. Every Shabbes, after the traditional meal, we would have tea with our relatives here. I could still taste the poppyseed cake they had served.

I climbed up on a pile of rubble. From there, for the first time, I could look into the ghetto. I was petrified. Behind the high barbed wire fence, gray, stooped forms were moving about. They walked slowly.

What a terrible sight! Everything went black, I gagged, and tears ran down my face. How I longed to see my mother's delicate features, to catch sight of my father's gentle, intelligent face.

By being with them, I wanted to cast a ray of light into the terrible darkness of their lives. I wanted to lessen their torment and their yearning for their son. If death had really been decreed for them, they should at least go to their final rest knowing that Shloimele was alive.

I was still standing on the pile of rubble, watching. Overwhelmed by what I saw, I felt my composure draining away. Everything became blurred. Who was I? What was I? For whom was I searching? And why? . . . I climbed down from the mound of rubble and walked over to the fence. There was a terrible emptiness around me, and it seemed as if my feet weren't touching the ground anymore, as if I were peering through a fog. Somehow I made out a huge yellow sign. It read "Residence Area for Jews—Entry Forbidden."

In four days my Hitler Youth comrades would be celebrating the "holy night" of Jesus' birth by singing carols under the blinking stars on their Christmas trees.

In grim contrast, my brothers and sisters, the Jews of the ghetto, moved about like lost shadows, ashen-faced and dressed in rags! I was overtaken by an ineffable grief. At that moment, nothing could have consoled me. For such a long time, for an eternity, I hadn't seen any Jews . . . except for the grotesque caricatures hanging on the walls of my classroom. Now I stood there as though hypnotized by their shuffling, dragging steps; they seemed to be desperately protecting a tiny flickering flame of life.

Behind the fence, a woman wearing a black-bordered gray shawl came walking along the curb. In the bitter cold she had difficulty merely setting one foot before the other.

A German soldier guards the entrance to the Lodz ghetto. The sign reads "Residence Area for Jews—Entry Forbidden." (Courtesy of Bundesarchiv.)

Could it be that I knew her? The more I stared at her the more convinced I became that it was my mother. Was it? Good God, I had come from so far away to see her. Had one of my guardian angels led her to me?

"Mama, Mama," I called out wordlessly, clinging to the fence. "I came to thank you, Mama, to show you that the terrible sacrifice you made wasn't in vain. Some day, when I'm grown up and have a child of my own, perhaps I will be able to appreciate the extent of your inner struggle and the deep sorrow you must have felt when you said to my brother, 'Isaac, take little Solly and lead him toward life!' They tore me from your side, but now I've come back to you—only a fence separates us. I don't see any children on the streets here; they must all be gone. . . . And you in your generosity, you saved me!"

The woman kept walking, turning the corner without even looking in my direction. I stood there, as if in a trance. I wanted to call after her, but a sort of safety catch in my brain kept me from doing it. I ran along the fence in the direction in which she had disappeared. How long did I run? How far? I don't know, but now I was standing at the entrance to the ghetto.

8

INTO THE GHETTO

The gate, made of heavy wooden boards, was open. I looked inside and saw the sign for Franziskanska Street. So close to my beloved parents! With every fiber of my being I was drawn to number 18, and now only a few houses separated me from realizing my dream. Several people, each of whom looked like my father or mother, were walking by. I stepped through the gate and walked up to them. The censor who controlled my life could no longer keep me from acting in a way that might endanger my own safety. Strangely invigorated, I thought I had come home; actually, I had lost touch with the real world. I was so upset and excited that I almost lost my self-control. There I stood in my black Hitler Youth winter uniform, facing imprisoned Jews I was forbidden to approach. Thoughts and emotions tumbled through my head in rapid succession. How can I possibly describe my feelings during those moments?

What if my mother is one of these people on the street, and what if she recognizes me and calls to me, "Shloimele, my son"? Would I throw my arms around her? No, I wouldn't; I'd pretend she was a stranger. Such an extraordinary incident could mean the end for both of us. What member of the Hitler Youth would go into the ghetto to kiss an old Jewish woman? A serious offense, punishable by death. If she were to speak to me, I would figure out a way to surreptitiously let her know who I really was. We would have to settle for an exchange of glances, hoping that some day we would see each other again. But would we be able to restrain ourselves?

I was completely absorbed in such thoughts when a man in a dark coat suddenly loomed up before me. He was wearing a visored cap with a white Star of David on it. His armband identified him as a Jewish ghetto policeman. He exuded an air of authority, but when our eyes met I could tell he was puzzled. We looked at each other, neither one of us saying a word. Behind me I heard someone ask in dialect-tinged German what I was doing here. A guard, evidently an ethnic German, came over. In the strictly structured German hierarchy, I, as a *Reichsdeutscher*, outranked him, and so he was not about to be rude. On my uniform shirt, above the swastika armband, he saw embroidered the words "*Bann* 468 Northern Lower Saxony, Brunswick." There was no need to identify myself further. "You must have lost your way," he said politely. "Only Jews live here. Didn't you know that?" I shrugged. "You are not allowed here. You could catch all kinds of diseases," he explained. "There are even epidemics here." I was "touched" by his concern for my health, and smiling, thanked him for his advice. I told him not to worry; I would follow his suggestion and leave. By this time, I had pulled myself together—Jupp was in charge again. In a matter-of-fact voice, I explained that I was just on my way through. He thought I meant I wanted to go to the non-Jewish quarter on the other side of the ghetto. "Take the streetcar," he said, "it passes right through the ghetto."

His suggestion intrigued me. I walked back through the gate and over to a nearby trolley stop. Amazingly, life was going on as usual all around the miserable ghetto in which hundreds of men, women, and children were dying of starvation and disease. Here, on the outside, the faces of the passersby gave no indication that they were affected by any of this. Shocking disinterest and indifference prevailed only a few yards from the ghetto walls. Even today the fact that people can get used to horror seems to me to be the most appalling and frightening reaction of which humankind is capable. The split I witnessed there, between two worlds— the one of abject wretchedness and the other of everyday normality—made a deep and lasting impression on me.

A loud clatter announced the approach of the streetcar. A few moments later, swaying around a curve, it turned into the street where I was waiting. The driver rang his bell, the wheels screeched, and the trolley came to a halt. I walked over to the car that was reserved for Germans, while the Poles who had waited with me had to board the one designated for them.

Instead of pushing my way into the car where I could find a seat among the other passengers, I remained standing near the front window. I knew that once we entered the ghetto I might lose control of myself. The Aryan travelers would surely not understand such behavior, and if they *did* understand, then what . . . ?

I stood just behind the driver, who threw me a quick glance to find out who was breathing down his neck; then he turned around to do his job. His uniform was clean and bore the insignia of the Litzmannstadt Transportation Department.

The heavy gate swung open; the streetcar crossed the ghetto boundary and then stopped. The Jewish policeman I had met before came toward us. Walking around the street-

A footbridge spanning the Lodz ghetto. Two "non-Jewish" streets traversed the ghetto. Forbidden to walk on them, Jews had to cross over them on wooden footbridges, while "non-Jewish" streetcars passed underneath. (Courtesy of Bundesarchiv.)

car, he locked all the doors with a special key—a security measure to prevent Jews in the ghetto from pushing onto the streetcar. Now the doors could be opened only from inside, and no German or Polish passenger would ever have considered opening the streetcar door for a Jew who wanted to save his life. We were moving again. The streetcar turned into Franziskanska Street, and I had to try hard to control the emotional storm raging within me. Still fresh on my mind was the horrendous and shocking contrast between the callous indifference on the outside and the atmosphere of annihilation and powerlessness that lay over everything behind this fence, a fence erected by bestial masters. I scarcely saw the house numbers. Looking searchingly straight ahead, I wanted to spot my parents' house as soon as it came into view. And there! There it was—the house I had so yearned to enter. I pressed my face hard against the trolley window: Stop, damned streetcar! Stop, so I can look a little longer. Maybe my mother's intuition that her son was nearby would draw her to one of the windows.

We had now reached the house at number 18. Nothing moved behind the dark windows. There would be no miracle. The trolley wheels kept turning. I sighed audibly. The driver turned around again and gave me a strange look.

I continued to stare through the window at the passersby. Perhaps I could spot a relative or a friend, or at least make eye contact with someone I knew. My gaze wandered from the people on the sidewalk, who seemed unreal, to the street, and from there to the windows of the houses we were passing.

None of the German passengers in the streetcar were looking out the windows. Evidently they didn't want to see or acknowledge this living testimony to the atrocities that were being committed here. Their faces were quite serene, as if apathy and criminality existed side by side within them. How could this be possible? Did all of them feel this way?

Were there no exceptions, did none of them feel conscience-stricken? Today they would say, "Our hearts were filled with sorrow concerning everything that happened there, but what could we have done?"

At a turn in the road, the driver slowed the streetcar, and suddenly I was confronted with the most depressing, the most shocking sight I have ever seen. Four men were pulling and pushing a rumbling cart loaded with corpses that had been haphazardly thrown onto it in a grotesque jumble. The bodies were covered with a tattered cloth that probably had once been a white sheet. The naked, emaciated limbs of the dead poked out from under this sheet. This terrible spectacle tore at my heart. The cart hit a pothole; dangling dead arms and legs bounced up and fell back down, bounced up, and then finally dropped back into their original positions; the cart continued down the street.

This is how they were taken to their graves. A terrible thought occurred to me: What if my mother were among these corpses . . . or my father . . . ?

God in heaven! Is there an answer, an explanation for what is happening in this place of horror to the faithful who believe in You?

I wanted to throw myself down on the floor of the trolley. I wanted to scream.

But the streetcar continued on its route, leaving my fellow Jews behind in their martyrdom. My eyes dimmed and everything around me blurred.

When we reached the exit of the ghetto, the streetcar stopped. Another Jewish policeman opened all the locked doors.

I got off at the first stop and wandered aimlessly through the streets. I had no place to go, nobody I could turn to. Four years had passed since I had left my parents and my home, but in all that time I had never felt such utter despair, such hopelessness. Was there no power on earth or in heaven that would make my dream come true and lead me into the arms of my parents? And could that happen even though I had been less than cautious in my quest? I hadn't come here to see and to die; I had come to find my parents and to go on living. I hadn't come here to be arrested and to make the Nazis' criminal handiwork easier for them. I hadn't come to surrender to the hangman who would have executed me with great pleasure. My mother would never forgive me such a sacrifice. It was my duty to go back to my life, to blend in with the hangmen, in order to fulfill her last wish: "You must stay alive."

9

RIDING THE STREETCAR

I decided to take the streetcar through the ghetto on each of the ten remaining days of my vacation. Perhaps my search would turn up something, someone. But I couldn't ignore the danger connected with this plan. I must not overdo these trips, or I might arouse the suspicion of an officer of the secret police or some other inquisitive person. The streetcar driver, obviously a Pole, might begin to wonder about the strange behavior of a Hitler Youth who kept taking the streetcar back and forth through the Jewish ghetto and always stayed close to the front window. What if he reported this behavior to the Gestapo? They would have been delighted to arrest me and start an investigation.

Naturally, in view of the precariousness of the situation I had to proceed with the greatest caution. I didn't know how often the streetcar made the trip through the ghetto, but more than two hours had gone by since I had gotten off. I crossed the street, joining others who were waiting there. I felt like an alien from another planet, like a migratory bird who's lost its flight companions. How could I get so close to my loved ones and yet not see them? Was the devil mocking me?

Helpless and shivering in the cold, I sat down on the bench at the trolley stop. All sense of time and space was gone. I was waiting for the streetcar so that I could take another look at "my house." When it finally arrived, I again went into the car reserved for the master race. We had the same driver, and again he looked at me curiously. After the door-locking ritual, the ghetto gates closed behind us. No luck this time either in my effort to see my parents.

For the trips to come I prepared a note in Polish on a scrap of paper. It read "To the Perel Family, Lodz Ghetto, 18 Franziskanska Street. Salek is alive. Watch the streetcars going by." I stuck the paper in my pocket, intending to drop it on the street at the first opportunity. Perhaps some sympathetic soul would give the message to my parents. But the paper stayed folded in my pocket. Finally I tore it into little pieces, afraid the note could end up in the wrong hands. It's no consolation, but even today I haven't forgiven myself for doing that.

That's how I passed the next few days. I slept sitting up on one of the benches in the train station. In the mornings I washed up in the public toilet, ate breakfast at the station buffet, and took the trolley—almost always with the same silent driver—to the ghetto. Although I tried not to attract his attention, I realized that I looked out of place in these surroundings and that he took note of me each time.

Between these trips I spent a lot of time on the familiar streets of Lodz. I wanted to visit the scenes of my childhood, just as I had done during my nostalgic trip to Peine. For hours every day I walked through the big city without meeting anyone with whom I could exchange a kind or friendly word.

In my loneliness, having temporarily lost touch with reality, I decided to visit my former classroom teacher, Mr.

Klemezki; even though he wasn't Jewish, I thought perhaps he would understand my dilemma and reassure me. This was a risky idea, childish and foolish, but I needed consolation; it didn't matter who provided it. Before the war, I had served as chairman of the Student League for Air Raid Precautions. Mr. Klemezki, an active participant in the league, had frequently invited me to his house. He lived on the Avenue of the Third of May, named in honor of Polish Constitution Day. Finding the building was easy. I climbed the stairs to the second floor and stopped at his apartment door. The kitchen was visible through a narrow window in the stairwell. He was sitting at the table, having a meal with his wife. I hesitated. Should I ring the bell? Suddenly an inner voice screamed, "Stop! Don't do it! Get out of here." I realized that even Mr. Klemezki, whom I used to trust, could now prove to be dangerous. Many people living under a military occupation government conform, and some turn into informers. In this case, it was merely the life of a Jewish child that was at risk—a sobering thought. I quickly ran down the stairs.

Several years after the war I got together with some of my former Lodz classmates. I told them about my intention at that time to look up Klemezki, hoping to find comfort and reassurance from him. One of the men said that after Poland was occupied by the Germans, Klemezki had turned into an enthusiastic Nazi collaborator. Of course, he would have had me arrested on the spot.

I walked toward 17 Zakontna Street, where I had lived up to the time of the traumatic parting from my parents and where the rest of my family had continued to live until they were driven behind ghetto walls. As I got closer to No. 17, memories flooded over me. I had my first date with a girl here, but now everything seemed strange and cold. The walls of the houses I passed and the familiar cobblestones were silent, impersonal witnesses to all that I had experienced on this street.

I had reached the front door of my house, a three-story corner building. I went in just as the porter came to the door. I knew him well; he had not changed and still wore the same old cap. I used to help him wash down the sidewalk and the yard with a hose. It was fun to press the rubber end of the hose to make the water spray in all directions. For a fraction of a second I thought of telling him who I was, of letting him in on my secret. But dismissing this stupid idea immediately, I carefully turned around to see that he wasn't following me. Then I confidently walked up the stairs to the first floor. Now I was standing in front of our old apartment door. An unfamiliar name appeared next to the doorbell. Someone had removed our *mezuzah*, but it had left a mark on the right doorpost.

What a beloved, homey place this had been for our happy family. In the evenings the house was filled with the sounds of joyful horseplay. My brother David was the joker in our family, and we almost died with laughter at his pranks. He especially liked to play tricks on us while we were eating. If he thought Mama had not given him enough soup, he would stick his finger in our sister Bertha's plate. She, of course, refused to finish it, leaving an extra portion for David. Mama would scold him a little, but then she herself had to laugh.

Isaac was the most serious and the strictest member of the family. He worked hard and loved order and neatness. He carefully supervised my progress in school and always made sure that I had done all my homework. . . . While we were living in Peine and later on in Lodz, he would make me go out for a walk and then, to test my powers of observation, he'd ask me to give him a detailed report of all the impressions I had collected on the street.

Bertha was a beautiful young woman; she taught me how to dance to music on the radio, at first slow foxtrots and tangos; later we did other dance steps. We also listened to the foreign radio stations. Whenever the local newspaper announced an upcoming broadcast of a speech by Hitler, there was anxious suspense. Hitler was an expert in whipping up the passions and emotions of the people, causing panic and terror in our family. In those speeches, he usually took the whole world to task, dramatically warning of privation, want, and devastation if the German people did not wake up and challenge the Treaty of Versailles. I can still hear his screaming voice today: "If the international Jewish financiers, in their efforts to amass more wealth and profit, should again succeed in drawing our people into a world war, it will mean the extermination of the Jewish race in Europe." And as he spoke, he was doing everything possible to make his prediction come true. Even in my worst nightmares I could not have imagined that I would one day be forced to swear an oath to Hitler and to belong to his host of followers.

I don't know how long I had been standing there. A lively mixture of voices came from inside the apartment. When I heard steps approaching from the other side of the door, I fled down the stairs and into the street. As I passed Aron Goretski's house, I looked into the courtyard where he and I used to play Ping-Pong. Of course, the Ping-Pong table was gone. Yet something in me simply refused to acknowledge and accept that such a deeply rooted world had been extinguished in the twinkling of an eye, without a survivor or a single witness to its existence.

The area around Zakontna Street held a magical charm for me, and I kept coming back here between trips through the ghetto, its shocking images still burning in my memory. The contrast with the carefree life of the people on the outside was heartbreaking.

Deep in thought and immersed in the past, I almost
didn't see a young woman who had stopped near me on the
sidewalk. With a charming smile, she stared at my black uniform. Worldly pleasures or romantic encounters were the
farthest thing from my mind, but still I turned to her and
asked why she was so curious about me.

"Are you really a member of the Hitler Youth in the
Reich?" she asked shyly.

"Yes," I said proudly, "in Brunswick. I'm from Northern
Lower Saxony." This surge of cockiness and the fact that I
could puff myself up a little in front of this pretty girl made
me feel better and somewhat less forlorn. She spoke German
with a Slavic accent; apparently she was an ethnic German. I
invited her to go for a walk. She agreed, and we continued to
stroll in the same direction in which I had been heading.
Evidently I was saying the right things, because the girl
seemed impressed; in turn, I was distracted for a little while
from my real self, which had been so shaken with pain.

My new friend kept looking at me with admiration. She
told me she was from the Ukraine and, as part of the German resettlement policy, had come to the west with her
family. Her father was with the army somewhere in the east,
and she, her mother, and a sister lived rent-free in a new
apartment they had been assigned on their arrival. She
claimed she had never been in Germany, but it had always
been her fondest wish to go there. And although she had met
Wehrmacht soldiers, she had never met a real live Hitler
Youth like me.

Young ethnic Germans admired the Hitler Youth movement and were hoping it would soon be set up in Lodz too.
The girl's enthusiasm was sincere, and I enjoyed talking to
her. It made me feel quite strange to think that, of all people,
fate had picked me to represent the young elite of the
Führer. So as not to disillusion her, and to play my role as a

representative of the Reich to the hilt, I pretended to be just as enthusiastic as she was.

I was inordinately happy to have found a young person to talk to and was pleased about the relationship developing between us. It was a small, gloriously colorful oasis in the midst of the bleak human desolation that surrounded me—a little joy in the midst of the tragedy I had been witness to in the last few days. In a way, it dispelled the gruesome impressions that threatened to kill any sensibility and hope I still had.

Our conversation continued on a cheerful note and with just a hint of flirtation. I longed for happiness, perhaps because my mind was thirsting for more positive feelings to counteract what I had seen in the ghetto. The tragic incidents and the sight of death during these vacation days had not dampened my joy for life. Some would say this was appalling.

It was getting dark. I said good-bye to the girl and hurried to my "hotel," the Kaliszki Railway Station. We had made a date for the following afternoon, and I looked forward to seeing her again.

I never succeeded in catching a glimpse of my parents in the ghetto. Jupp, on the other hand, had been successful—almost gloriously successful—in contrast to Solly, who was inconsolable and drowning in sorrow.

After the war I found out that at the time of my visit to the ghetto, most of the Lodz Jews already had been sent to Auschwitz. Those who were still in the ghetto were from nearby areas and they too would soon be deported.

The next day, after again taking the streetcar through the ghetto, I walked to the spot where the girl and I had agreed to meet. She was already there and made no attempt to hide her pleasure at seeing me again. We took another long walk to the edge of the city, and at one point our hands touched. My heart beat faster, and I felt alive again. Holding hands can mean, can symbolize, a lot of things. I shall always remember that sensual touch.

We took up our conversation of the day before. Youthful enthusiasm can quickly inspire a warm relationship to develop between strangers. The wave of sympathy that flowed from her toward me was touching, even though it was based on a fundamental misunderstanding. Hadn't she been taught to hate what I really was? Still, her feelings for me helped to soften my grief.

On the way back she surprised me. Shyly she invited me to celebrate New Year's Eve, the following night, at her house. At first I was evasive; I was in no mood to celebrate. On the other hand, I wasn't trying to be abstemious, and so I accepted her invitation; it seemed sincere. I asked her where she lived. And I was dumbfounded when she said, "I live near the place where I first talked to you, in the big house on the corner, at 17 Zakontna Street." Almighty God! Would life's provocations never stop? To be invited to the house of my once happy but later destroyed childhood! To eat, to drink, and to dance there, when every tile and floorboard reminded me of David's laughter, Isaac's love for me, Bertha's tango lessons, and, above all, my dear parents! Undeniably, wanting to go to a party in that house was completely irrational. But my wish to spend some time with a family and to push my bitterness into the background for a while was the deciding factor.

She hadn't mentioned the floor and the number of the apartment in which I would be celebrating the arrival of the new year of 1944. The thought that it might be in our confiscated apartment drove me wild. I would be confronted by material remnants of my past. I would be walking on the floorboards that I remembered from my childhood—this time as an invited guest, a welcomed stranger—and I was afraid.

Without knowing it, the girl was a bridge between my past and my present. She had no inkling of what her invitation meant to me. I would never have forgiven myself if I had turned it down, since it would be an extraordinary journey into the past, a celebration and at the same time an hour of mourning. I couldn't wait for the moment to arrive.

This encounter between Jupp and Solly was full of antitheses and contradictions. Joy and sorrow would clash in the house that was once my home.

"On what floor is your apartment?" I asked.

"Second floor; it's the door on the right. Don't forget to come!"

I barely heard what she was saying. So the party wouldn't be in our apartment after all, but rather on the floor above. I was disappointed that I wouldn't be able to touch the walls that probably still exuded the aroma of my mother's cooking. I had been invited to what had been the apartment of our Jewish neighbors whose son had gone to school with me. We had done our homework together in that apartment. Now they were all in the ghetto or in Auschwitz. And I had agreed to attend a party in what used to be their home, a party given by people who had only recently been installed there by their Nazi murderers.

This truth grew to enormous proportions and threatened to explode.

I tried to remain calm and to see the young woman merely as an innocent participant in a tragic, perplexing drama.

The next day the sidewalks were crowded with people hurriedly making last-minute preparations for New Year's Eve celebrations. As I strolled among them, I looked directly at them as if to say, "Today I'm just like you. Tonight you won't find me huddled on a bench in that damned train terminal." To be carrying on this unspoken dialogue with the passersby made me feel less alone. I'd become quite stubborn in recent years, and it wasn't easy to spoil my good mood.

That evening, all spruced up, I made my way to the party. I wasn't curious as to who the other guests were; probably they were relatives or friends of the girl and her family. One of them turned out to be a *Wehrmacht* soldier whose unit was stationed nearby. He and I were the only "genuine" Germans there, and as such we were treated as guests of honor. I was bursting with pride and self-assurance.

The soldier and I talked the same language. I didn't tell him that I was a front-line veteran myself, and I concealed the fact that I was an ethnic German who had been "incorporated" into the Reich. He thought I was a real German from Brunswick, and that's exactly how I wanted him to think of me, now and in the future. He cursed the Russians, and complained about their barbarous use of dumdum bullets in violation of the Geneva Convention. These bullets exploded inside the victim's body after he was shot, causing dreadful wounds. He had been hit in the thigh, and the wound had taken eight months to heal. That was why, for the time being, he was serving in an anti-aircraft unit behind the lines.

The buffet table was overflowing with food in spite of the prevailing shortages. Alcohol—homemade brandy and wine—and a whole series of dishes were served freely. By the time midnight approached, spirits were quite high.

There was singing and dancing to music from an old record player. I invited my hostess to dance. Some of the people were laughing so hard, tears came to their eyes, but my tears were tears of mourning. Bertha had taught me the tango I was dancing now. I shut my eyes, held my partner close, and abandoned myself to a flood of tormenting memories. She interpreted this as affection for her. This kind young woman had made it possible for me to be my real self and to slide back into the forbidden past while Jupp enjoyed the pleasures of a flirtation.

A few minutes before the stroke of midnight, the dance of dreams about my former world was interrupted. We all linked arms and danced a festive and joyous round in honor of the Führer and victory. I joined in too. But my hopes were not for the same victory. I kept my short prayers to myself. What a lucky thing that thoughts and feelings can remain silent and invisible. The party could continue.

Who could have known that fate would lead me back to the house I had left four years earlier, there to dance and shed some tears! While my family was imprisoned in the ghetto, I was "amusing" myself in the apartment of my former friends and neighbors. The furniture they had left behind bore silent witness.

My time in Lodz was coming to an end, and I would leave this fateful place with the most contradictory feelings. But I knew I had to obey the demands of the present and go on with my life.

The last trips I made through the ghetto only caused me more disappointment. Disconsolate, I lost all hope of seeing my parents. Once or twice, I saw Jupp's girlfriend again, and then we parted. I also bade a silent farewell to the odd streetcar driver—all this time I had not exchanged a single word with him, leaving him to wonder about my nervous trips through the ghetto.

In Israel, not long ago, at a meeting of Jewish survivors of the Lodz ghetto, I met a sprightly, remarkably vital old man named Binem Koppelmann. He told me that he lived in Sweden most of the time but came to Israel twice a year to stay in a house he owned in Savyon. The talk turned to the Shoah. *He told me of his wanderings, of his life in the Lodz ghetto, and of his arrival in Auschwitz on one of the last transports. He spoke nonstop and passionately, paying no attention to my questions. When he said he had been a motorman on a Lodz streetcar, I was finally able to interrupt him, "But how was it possible that a Jew was permitted to leave the ghetto?" He said he was the only one to be given this privilege. He had worked at the Elektrogerätewerk [Electrical Appliance Works] AEG in Berlin when he was young, he said, and when he told them of the experience he had acquired there, the German authorities issued him a special permit to drive the trolley.*

During another slight pause in his avalanche of words I told him that I too had ridden through the ghetto on the streetcar, hiding behind a Hitler Youth uniform.

The old man looked shocked and fell silent. He was frowning with concentration, and I sensed that he was rummaging about in his memory, trying to recall something. He looked at me for a long time and then asked hesitantly, "So, it was you? I was the motorman on that streetcar. Were you really the Hitler Youth who stood behind me, day after day? I was afraid of you and didn't have the nerve to ask you to explain why you kept taking the trolley back and forth. It seemed so odd, so unusual. But I'd never have thought that you were a Jew."

"And I thought you were Polish," I said, "a suspicious Pole who was trying to find out what I was up to."

After these ten days of vacation, I was quite confused and disappointed as I started heading back to school. This time I took any old seat on the train, and I didn't read a newspaper. I was shattered and no longer knew where I belonged. I couldn't remember where I had been, I didn't know what was in store for me. Where was my home? Which was my homeland? Who was I? My mind was in total disarray.

Not long ago a woman asked me why I hadn't tried to sneak into the ghetto and share my parents' fate. I told her that an inner mechanism had charted my path. I felt that I had to obey its commands.

10

WAR'S END

When I got back to school, I saw that nothing had changed. The sky had not fallen, and life continued on its course. The war was entering its fifth year, and everybody was firmly convinced of a final German victory.

My schoolmates and I were happy to see one another again. They all had interesting stories to tell. I contributed what I could to this exchange of experiences, evading all embarrassing questions. This time I had to try hard to invent fictional adventures. The chasm separating reality from fantasy was too deep. . . .

But soon the strict school discipline and the familiar surroundings took over, and I was back on track again.

In class they continued to praise the glorious changes Germany was bringing about in the world. Even the construction of a memorial commemorating the first of the former boarding school students killed at the front could not change this attitude. They were not troubled by the fact that Mussolini had been toppled and that Italy no longer wanted to be allied with Germany. We were told that Germany had gotten rid of an ally who had always been unreliable. We had the impression that "victory by the sword could be achieved" without allies. . . . Even the latest assassination attempt against Hitler did not dampen the ardent enthusiasm and steadfast faith.

A few days later, on movie screens all over Germany, there were films of the injured Hitler, showing him surrounded by the faithful—men who were still quite ready to follow his insane path, even now. Death raged on, and millions more were exterminated.

We were called together for a briefing about the assassination attempt on Hitler. The *Bannführer* expressed his indignation, saying the gang of traitors who had conspired to kill the Führer would get their just punishment. He urged us to stand firmly on the side of National Socialism, and we swore to do so by raising our right arms and singing the Nazi anthem. We were also shown excerpts from a film taken during the trials of the conspirators in the *Volksgerichtshof* [People's Court]. It showed how they were harassed and badgered and, finally, sentenced. I remember one sequence in which General von Witzleben stood before the judges holding up his trousers because they had taken his belt away. When the presiding judge ordered him to stand at attention, the general's trousers fell down, revealing his underpants. The spectators in the courtroom found this amusing, and they laughed.

A few of the accused were hanged on meat hooks—like pigs after the slaughter.

Life returned to normal. But toward the end of July 1944 I was ordered to report to the school administration building. There they informed me that a summons for me had arrived. I was to pick up some official papers at a particular office in the Brunswick police headquarters.

I became tense and alert. I had no idea what this was about. Any official inquiry was bound to make my precarious situation more dangerous. That night I woke up several times, wondering what it might mean, conjuring up prospects, one more threatening and horrible than the next.

After class the following day, I gathered the few documents I had and started out on a path that might end in my death. If they discovered my Jewish background, I hoped that they would at least be merciful and kill me immediately. I consoled myself with the thought that perhaps they would take me to Lodz, where I might see my parents again. The idea of being among other Jews in the ghetto seemed preferable to my constant loneliness.

As I entered the police station, I felt shaky even though I had already accepted the possibility that my life would now change. For a brief moment I stood there, trying to pull myself together, to prepare myself mentally. Then I knocked on a door that said "Domestic Affairs, German Citizenship Department."

A voice called out, "Come in."

I walked in, erect, bold, ready to do battle. A civil service employee wearing a party badge was sitting at a desk. I threw back my shoulders and let go with an especially snappy *"Heil Hitler!"* He briefly replied in kind and asked me to sit down. I handed him my summons. "Hmmm," he said, and began to leaf through a file on his desk. Thanks to the constant practice I had had, I managed to keep my facial muscles under control, to conceal my apprehension, but it took a mighty effort. The official took his time, calmly reading through the documents without saying a word. Every minute that passed was nerve-racking. Finally he raised his head and asked, "What region does the name Perjell come from?"

"From Lithuania, the East, from the Baltic region," I replied without hesitation, remembering the name expert at the front in Minsk.

"Right, right. You're probably right," he said, and he sounded convinced. "Well now, where is your certificate of

[Aryan] ancestry? It seems to be missing. We need it to complete our file on you."

I proudly pulled out the precious document that confirmed I had lost all my identification papers and held it out to him. He nodded. "Yes, good. This is a very respectable document. But we need something official, an authorized document to complete your file. You will have to write to your hometown, Grodno, and request a copy of your certificate of German ancestry. "Do it right away," he said laconically with a glacial laugh, "otherwise we'll have to resort to the usual measures. . . ."

"Yessir, I'll write a letter to Grodno this very day," I said, wondering all along if there might be another way out.

The front lines were collapsing, the Allies were proceeding with their liberation of France, and here were these Germans, still worried about foreign elements infiltrating their master race! We exchanged a few more polite words and parted with the usual Hitler salute. I ran down the steps of the police headquarters, gasping for fresh air. After breathing deeply, I felt somewhat better. What to do? Of course, I wouldn't write to Grodno—no ethnic German named Josef Perjell had ever been born there.

Strange, but apparently it hadn't occurred to the police official that he could write to Grodno himself—instead, he had left it up to me to do so. What a relief to know that I had a month to find a way out of this predicament. I had the feeling I was free, but free like someone who's been sentenced to death and is in a cell without bars and no lock on the door.

I didn't let anybody at the HJ school know how worried I was. Instead I decided to visit the Latsches the following Sunday so that I could talk to Leni's mother about this ominous situation and ask for her advice.

But it never came to that. Again my guardian angel took a hand. That night Brunswick was bombed. Up to then the Allied planes had just flown over the city without dropping a single bomb; all the air raids were targeted for Berlin. As a consequence, the local anti-aircraft defenses had become somewhat lax. In addition, a fairly plausible rumor had it that the city was being spared. The scuttlebutt was that the British royal family was related to the House of Brunswick and wanted the city saved so that the British could take possession of it undamaged. This rumor persisted stubbornly until the night dozens of flares, so-called Christmas trees, lit up the sky, turning night into day. A rain of bombs transformed the city into a pile of rubble. Brunswick was burning. The exploding bombs surprised us and caused a general panic that was even worse than the one I had experienced in Grodno. How fickle fate is! Again I was at the mercy of air attacks, but this time the bombs were fortunate for me. There were screams of terror and contradictory commands were issued, but all were drowned out by the noise of the bursting bombs and the roar of the British bombers.

The building that housed the German Citizenship Department now lay in ruins. It had been totally destroyed, and one would have searched the rubble in vain for any surviving files, including mine, which was awaiting the confirmation from Grodno. Everything had gone up in flames. I sent a prayer of thanks to heaven for the anonymous bombardier who had aimed so superbly. And I thought, There you are, Shloimele, now they won't bother you any more with investigations into your ancestry! After the all-clear, we were ordered to join the "rubble detachments." We had had practice with this type of work because we had helped out doing relief work in nearby Hanover, which was bombed frequently. I was ready to go out there with my classmates to do my duty. Mostly we made coffee and sandwiches, handing them out on street corners.

My parents had raised me to give my all when it came to saving human lives. A human being was a human being; it didn't matter to me what his or her sex, age, or origin was. In that regard I had no moral conflicts. Every individual wounded and buried under the rubble of a house had a right to receive my help. It did not matter what he had done previously or what he would have done to me had he found out who I was. At times like these, Jupp took over, and like everybody else, I rushed around and helped in the rescue operations.

In the three years I spent at the National Socialist school, I constantly tried to be one of the best students, and I easily succeeded. Completely wrapped up in my studies, I was driven by enormous energy. On the other hand, I knew how to stay away from anything that could have depressed me or could have upset me. And so I have to admit that now and then, I forgot my past completely.

My life was like a clock with a pendulum that swung to two extremes. At one end was the temporary, false life that had been forced on me. At the other, my genuine, deeply rooted but concealed life.

The pendulum swung irregularly. Most of the time it hung in Jupp's world. Then, for a time, it would move to the other end. Returning from Solomon's world, it would first undergo a brainwashing before swinging all the way over to Jupp's.

Sometimes I had trouble knowing in which personality I was lodged. My double existence confused me, and there were times I couldn't really tell which role I preferred to play. As a result, I was full of enthusiasm for the victories of "our Fatherland, our Greater Germany." We waited eagerly for news of military victories, and I didn't hold back from displaying my joy when there were announcements of profoundly heroic deeds. With each announcement of a major success, there was cheering and jubilation and we hugged each other. I too would rejoice at every step that brought us closer to "final victory." I wasted no time thinking of my primary goal or my future after the final defeat of the Allies, and so I avoided inner conflicts. It wasn't a deliberate or imposed resignation, it was just a relatively sure way to survive and to triumph over the murderous Nazi regime.

Frequently we had Imminent Air Raid Alert 15, meaning that enemy aircraft were fifteen minutes' flying time away from Brunswick. The rules were that we had to drop whatever we were doing when we heard the air raid sirens and hurry to the air raid shelter. But the planes flew overhead frequently without dropping any bombs. And so we relaxed our vigilance. Apathy and carelessness spread. There were some "brave" guys who decided simply to ignore the danger and stay in their rooms. Then the inevitable happened. One beautiful sunny morning the radio announced Imminent Air Raid Alert 15, and this time the bombs fell and hit our residence. Everybody ran as though demented to the air raid shelters. During this head-over-heels race one of my best friends, Björn Folvik, a member of the young guard of the Norwegian Quislings, was killed. I had just enough time to reach safety. Deeply saddened by Björn's death, I wrote a poem, on the spur of the moment, in honor of my dead friend. It began like this:

He lies there, dead on the grass,
his face turned upward,
as if he wanted to say:
For the holy Fatherland,
Forward, comrades! Forward!

Nun liegt er tot auf dem Rasen
mit dem Gesicht nach oben
als wollt er sagen:
Für's heilige Vaterland
vorwärts Kameraden!

I behaved and talked just like the others. I was a member of the group, body and soul—in spirit as well as in appearance. Today I see it clearly: my behavior in those days flew in the face of all logic. In retrospect, that's hard to understand and to judge. But that's the way it was.

One day, during the race education class, my two identities collided and I was thrown off balance. The teacher called on me to explain why the Jews had to be exterminated. Only Satan could have asked such a question, and only he could have expected an answer from someone with my background. Taken aback and stunned, I went up to the podium. Wild with rage and disgust, I strained at the same time to collect all my faculties to survive this test. I had to wring new strength I didn't know I possessed from my soul. Here the past was clashing with the present, and the whole unhappy paradox was sharply revealed. To pick me, of all people, to speak on this subject! I repeated all that had been drummed into us in previous classes. No outward sign betrayed my inner tortures. I had the impression the racist teacher was satisfied with my recitation; he probably gave me an excellent grade.

The situation at the war front was getting worse daily, but the mood among the civilian population was fairly good. It got even better in response to some encouraging rumors about a secret weapon that would decide the outcome of the war in favor of the Germans. The scuttlebutt had it that it was "five minutes to noon," and that the Führer would soon give the signal to launch a weapon whose destructive power was unique in military history. After the war I heard that Nazi Germany had been working feverishly on the development of an atomic bomb.

In spite of the changed situation at the front, there was a peculiar air of indifference at the HJ school. On June 6, 1944, a second front had opened with the Allied landings in Normandy. At the same time the Russian army was achieving decisive victories in a dramatic breakthrough. The Soviets were liberating territories the Nazis had conquered;

marching across the Polish border, they inflicted heavy casualties on the *Wehrmacht.*

The outcome of the war had been decided, more or less. But in school we continued dreaming our Big Power dreams, and the changing circumstances didn't make me vacillate. I was deeply involved in a world that had been forced upon me, my reasoning powers had finally been completely anesthetized, and my mental faculties were so befogged that no ray of reality could penetrate. I continued to feel just like one of them. Even the adventurous and dangerous last-ditch measures employed by the Germans seemed right and proper. I no longer worried about what was going to happen to me after the defeat of the *Wehrmacht.* While the German Reich was already in its death throes, I was still participating in desperate rescue efforts. We joined the *Volkssturm,* the "spontaneously" formed squads of children, Hitler Youths, women, and old men—anyone who could still hold a weapon—to defend the borders of the fatherland against the approaching foe.

In early 1945, in the forests on the outskirts of Brunswick, we were trained in the use of a new anti-tank weapon, an anti-tank rocket launcher called *Panzerfaust.* By then my classmates already considered themselves old warriors. . . . Finally we had been given a weapon to use. It was simple and effective, but it was dangerous to handle. When you pushed the trigger to fire the *Panzerfaust,* a long flame shot out the back. Several of my cohorts suffered severe burns.

The newspapers published photographs showing Hitler awarding medals for bravery to Hitler Youths fighting in the *Volkssturm.* I was part of a unit formed to go to the western front. Because of my previous front-line experience, I was appointed platoon leader [*Zugführer*]. We were supposed to guard road and highway bridges and help the *Wehrmacht* in the destruction of enemy tanks. After all, this young Viking generation could not permit foreigners to penetrate the beloved fatherland. On the way to the front we saw massive troop movements heading in the opposite direction. For the first time I heard my brothers-in-arms pointedly remark, "They're clearing out and going home. The war's over for them."

Then why didn't I crawl out of my shell now that the wind had changed direction? Instead I just sat around, gloomy, confused, and powerless. I don't know what mental block kept me from getting up and pulling out. The front was pretty far away, but you could definitely hear the sounds of battle. For me the hour of truth had struck.

In spite of my emotional and ideological confusion, I was not about to launch a single grenade at an "enemy" tank. I had not forgotten that these were not my enemies. I wanted to meet them at last, to welcome them. From deep down, a long-dead hope arose. It was only a faint hope, but strong enough gradually to dissolve the fog that had surrounded me in the preceding years, the same mist that had shrouded my true origins and protected me.

This awakening did not come overnight. The constant tension from my years of fighting for survival did not let up all at once, but gradually it began to fade. I couldn't just peel off the Nazi skin in which I had lived and survived. It wasn't that simple. It had become my own skin.

April 21, 1945 was my twentieth birthday.

Six years had passed since I started this lunatic existence. For four of these years I had been robbed of my identity, I had become someone else.

The day before had been Hitler's birthday. We had listened to Joseph Goebbels' customary speech to the German people in which, as always on this day, Hitler and all of Germany were celebrated. I clearly remember the last sentences of that speech. With a marked change in the tone of his voice, Goebbels said, "If we Germans lose the war, then the goddess of justice is a money-grabbing whore, and we Germans will no longer deserve to live on this earth."

Tremendous events took place that night, the night between the defeated Führer's birthday and my twentieth. The end of the war was close. It was the most beautiful birthday present I, and the whole world, could ever have imagined!

The curtain fell. But now another curtain was rising. The isolation, the self-repudiation of the young Jew Solomon, son of Azriel, was over.

11

LIBERATION

During that momentous night I was suddenly awakened from a light sleep by a painful blow from a rifle butt. Orders in a foreign language were being shouted.

The American army had stormed our camp without meeting the slightest resistance. A squad of soldiers ordered us to stand against the wall. They took our weapons and all the equipment we had left and stacked it in a big pile outside. I watched as an American soldier grabbed my camera out of my backpack; now it was his. I didn't dare protest or show any other reaction.

"Up against the wall, Nazis!" they yelled until all of us were standing in a row with our arms crossed above our heads. I lined up with the others, my back to the wall. This was a new, unfamiliar reality, a hallucination. Near me, someone whispered that we were about to be shot. Soldiers, drunk with victory, who still had fresh memories of the horrors of war, could easily be carried away by a thirst for revenge.

And so I found myself confronting new "enemy" soldiers, very much like four years ago in a field near Minsk.

Why was it that then I was able to gather together all my courage and tell the German guard, "I'm an ethnic German"? Now I was petrified, unable to yell, "Don't shoot! I'm not one of them; I'm Jewish; it's really true." Instead I stood there, without making a sound. I was caught in my thick, tough Hitler shell and I couldn't free myself.

How ironic it would be, I thought, if on my birthday— at the very moment the bells of freedom were ringing—I were shot by the liberators.

My twisted life story would pass into oblivion. I wanted to yell, but I was afraid. The words just wouldn't come. I was in shock and couldn't find a way out.

Luckily they weren't about to shoot us. It probably never occurred to the American soldiers to take revenge on us. They saw us as misled youngsters and wanted only to scare us.

For a long hour we stood there, facing the menacing rifle barrels, until all the inspections and confiscations were concluded. Then most of the Americans left while a small group stayed behind to guard us.

We were ordered to remove all Nazi insignia from our uniforms; from that time on it was forbidden by the Allies to wear them. I quickly discarded all the sports badges I had earned as well as my Hitler Youth belt and shoved them as far away from me as I could.

But who was I now? Suspended between unfamiliar, undefined realms, I had no firm ground under my feet and no home to which I could return. I still did not know my true identity; it just didn't exist at that moment. Freedom was incomprehensible to me; I had forgotten what it felt like.

The next day our brief stint as prisoners ended. We went off in all directions, each going his own way, joining countless refugees who were roaming the countryside, searching for their scattered families. So far I had not told anyone that I was Jewish. First I wanted to make my way back to my school in Brunswick to pick up my things and to collect my wits. I wanted to think about what had happened, to come to grips with the fact that the dark years of hiding behind a lie were now at an end. I had to accustom myself to the light of a new world. And so, completely confused, I started out toward a new life. I got hold of a bicycle and pedaled to Brunswick. There were thousands of people on the roads—refugees trying to find their way mingled with defeated, discouraged, and exhausted *Wehrmacht* soldiers. And everywhere, the victorious Allies. A chaotic mass of people in all kinds of vehicles, makeshift carts, bicycles, or on foot. . . .

What to do first? What would my future be like, and how would it tie in with what had gone before? Would I be able to put my broken life together again—to build a new life on such an unstable foundation? Naturally, I had shed my borrowed identity, but I still hadn't found my true self. I was cycling to no-man's-land. Something had come to an end, but there was no new beginning.

I stopped to rest in a ditch by the side of the road and pulled from my knapsack some food we had been given at the front. While I was eating, I saw Germans passing by, heading in different directions. I watched prisoners of war who, under close guard, were being sent to collection and distribution centers. The tables were turned. The proud master race with its unlimited power seemed to have reached the end of its tether.

As I got closer to Brunswick, I heard that the city had been occupied and the population had been forced to hang white flags out their windows as signs of surrender. I pedaled my bicycle with renewed energy and, tired and panting, I arrived in the conquered city. And indeed, white flags were flying everywhere. Huge posters had been pasted on building walls by the American occupation forces, announcing clearly and unequivocally that any citizen found in possession of a weapon or Nazi insignia, or anyone who violated the curfew, would be shot.

I hurried to get to my former school, since it was already close to curfew time. Many people were standing next to the hedge that surrounded the school. These were the workers from the east who had been forced to work in the Volkswagen plant. Now they were free. They had moved out of the cramped barracks encircled by barbed wire into the spacious rooms of the school dormitories. So I couldn't go back in to get my things.

Since I had no choice, I decided to go to the camp the forced laborers had once occupied. It wasn't far, and I managed to get there a few minutes before the curfew. I slipped through the barbed wire and disappeared into one of the barracks. There I collapsed onto a cot. There was no one to take me under his wing now. I was all alone, alone with the past. This was a completely different kind of loneliness, not any easier to bear. I had left the defeated Germans, but I was not one of the victors—a bitter and unique situation. Something important within me was oozing away, drop by drop. My senses were not as acute as they once were; I had lost the ability to find on-the-spot answers for everything; and my strong will and determination were gone. Even though they had fulfilled their purpose, I needed them now more than ever before.

It was getting dark; I ate a bit from the last reserves in my backpack. Then I curled up and fell into a deep sleep. Sleep was an escape, a way to evade, to delay facing the future. I needed time to recover.

Long before, I had left my *Wehrmacht* unit reluctantly, feeling sad. And now after three years as a Hitler Youth— seemingly leading a normal life but constantly struggling to survive—I felt an enormous weariness for the first time.

One spark of hope remained—my conviction that I could somehow work things out had not quite vanished. That was enough to make me get up the next morning to greet the new day and to make a new start.

I remembered a girl I used to go out with in Brunswick. She lived nearby, and I decided to look her up. I went up the wooden steps of her house and knocked. It took a while before she opened the door and cautiously peered out. She said she was glad to see me and asked how I was. She said, with some embarrassment, that she was sorry but she couldn't ask me to come in because she had company. Would I come back in the afternoon? Through the half-open door I could see a uniform carelessly thrown over a chair. Surprised and dismayed, I left immediately. You? And so soon?

I would visit Mrs. Latsch and her daughter Leni that afternoon. Meanwhile, I returned to the deserted barracks. In a big field near the barracks I ran into some Poles and Russians. "Hey, look at that German guy prowling around," one of them said to his companions. They came toward me, cursing and threatening. I tried to speak to them in Russian, to tell them that they were wrong, I wasn't German. But why should they believe me when I, Solly, was still walking around in Jupp's uniform? They beat me up even though I kept yelling, "I'm Jewish!" Finally I was able to get away and headed f   Town Hall on the main street to pick up the
          's I was entitled to. I was hungry and wanted
       to eat.
          ; full of pedestrians. A man who looked ut-
          ne toward me. His head was shaved and
          ·ison clothes. On his chest he wore a col-
          1d a number sewn on it and below that
          I looked at him and continued on my
          ...g a few steps I stopped. *Jew?* Could that
       .. ı felt a pang: had other Jews survived? I knew of
none besides myself.

The spark of my heritage came alive and started to burn in me. I turned around and ran to catch up with the man. Planting myself in front of him, I looked at him wide-eyed, as though he were a supernatural apparition.

With incredible naïveté, I asked him, "Excuse me, sir, are you really Jewish?" He gave me a bleak stare. Naturally, he couldn't have known that I was Jewish too, since I was still wearing my uniform. Dark spots on the threadbare material left no doubt that only a short while ago the accursed and incriminating Nazi insignia had still been there.

I wanted to grab him and shake him to convince him that we had something in common. From the most remote corner of my memory came the most beautiful and solemn words: "*Shema Yisroel*, Hear O Israel."

He seemed to believe me when I put my arms around him and whispered, "I'm a Jew too. My name is Solomon Perel."

That was a decisive moment. The strange world I had been forced to accept fell away. I had reached my goal. I put my head on his shoulder and wept tears of joy and thanksgiving. I had found new strength. He also was swept up by my emotions, and his eyes sparkled just like mine. This man who meant so much to me was Manfred Frenkel. Originally from Brunswick, he had been liberated from Auschwitz after having been transported there from the Lodz ghetto.

I immediately asked, "Did you by any chance meet any of the Perels in the ghetto?"

"Yes," he said, "for a while I worked at the freight railway station in Lodz, and in my work detail there was a Jew named David Perel."

"That's my brother!" I cried. I was sure this was the first milestone on the road that would lead me to my family. Unfortunately, he could provide no other details, but he was the first one to tell me about the place of horror called Auschwitz, and the gas chambers, the crematoria, and the atrocities that were committed there.

Our conversation left me speechless. I had lived among the Nazis for four years and never heard about any of this. How could I not have realized that they would implement in the most gruesome ways what they had taught us about liquidating the Jews, "this people of parasites and bloodsuckers"? Had my German classmates heard about the Nazi crimes from their parents and just not talked about it? Had there been a conspiracy of silence? Our teachers knew the horrible dimensions of the mass murders, but under the generally prevailing conditions of concealment they didn't discuss this in class. They contented themselves with presenting only the theoretical desirability of the eradication of the Jews.

During those years I had often met forced laborers on the streets of Brunswick. Patches on their clothes showed where they came from and distinguished them from the local population. I used to watch the weekly newsreels at the movies, but not once did they show people wearing prisoners' clothing. Presumably, the majority of Germans in the Third Reich had an inkling of the dimensions of the extermination operation, but the subject never came up in conversations when I was present. In all the years I lived among them, as one of them, I did not hear the faintest rumor or the tiniest hint about genocide. The "final solution" was never mentioned on the radio or in the newspapers. Or could it be that my eyes and ears were stopped up? Was this how I had let myself be taken in?

In contrast to the official silence about the extermination camps, Goebbels' propaganda had made a big to-do about the discovery of a mass grave of Polish officers near Katyn. "How can the world just shut its eyes to this massacre committed by the Bolsheviks?" was the cynical question asked by the murderers of millions of human beings. They never mentioned their own crimes. Although I learned about the Nazi racial theories in the ideological hothouse of the HJ school, my mind refused to acknowledge that these theories were already being applied in the various death camps. Manfred Frenkel was the first to open my eyes.

The profound sorrow I felt then has been with me ever since. When I took the streetcar through the ghetto all those times, how could I not have realized that the people I saw on the streets would not stay there, that the ghetto was just one of the links in the long chain of transports to extermination!

As I look back today, it strikes me that I had seen only adults in the ghetto, not a single child. At the time, this didn't particularly disturb me; I didn't ask myself what it might mean. The system I was entangled in sharpened my senses, but it also anesthetized them.

I felt deeply depressed during the nights I spent, only half asleep, in the abandoned camp. The liberated people I saw were all beaming, since they knew that in a few weeks they would be going back to their own countries, to cities and villages where they would return to their homes and hearths and take up their normal lives. But I . . . I had no place to go. For me, everything had been destroyed.

I remembered *Hatikvah*, the hymn of hope I had learned in the Gordonia Club in Lodz. Now I sang the song to myself, and it comforted me.

One day I heard voices coming from the adjoining barracks. I sneaked closer and saw two young Soviet women bending over a cot. They were nursing a Russian laborer who, on a binge, had consumed huge amounts of methyl alcohol. His insides were burning up, and he had lost consciousness. Carried away in his celebration of the liberation, the poor man had paid a terrible price.

I knew one of those girls, a beautiful young woman with Slavic features. We had formed a clandestine friendship while I was working in the Volkswagen workshops, the insignia of a Hitler Youth *Scharführer* still sparkling on my chest. We had talked together in Russian quite a few times in spite of the fact that this was forbidden. It had been a pleasant relationship. Now all those restrictions had been lifted, and we could speak honestly about the past.

Tshaika Gallina Jakovna (wearing head cloth), the Ukrainian *Ostar-beiter* with whom I formed a clandestine friendship in the Volkswagen workshops.

I have carefully saved her address and the photo she gave me as a souvenir. I had intended to visit her in Tevlinski and ask for Comrade Tshaika Gallina Jakovna at the Sovkohoz Karl Marx as soon as the political situation between Israel and the Soviet Union permitted it, but I have not gone there. I had said good-bye to her as Josef Perjell, the German, and when the time had come to tell her the truth, I didn't. To this day I don't know why.

A brief stop at the Latsch family's home gave me the chance to see Leni for the last time. Her mother had already told her my secret. We were happy to see each other again, went out together, and then said farewell. The friendship of the BDM girl and the Hitler Youth was over.* I corresponded with her mother for several years until she died. Leni eventually became a ballet dancer and married our mutual friend, Ernst M., who had worked for the Gestapo. They emigrated to Canada.

---

* I should mention at this point that, unlike the story depicted in the film *Europa, Europa*, Leni had not become pregnant. That had happened to a mutual friend of ours. The infant was adopted by an SS family.

1 2

FROM BRUNSWICK
TO ISRAEL

And then I left Brunswick. Besides the hard times, I had also had many happy experiences there, and so I had mixed feelings about the city. I remember the painful moments as well as the pleasant ones—they are jumbled together higgledy-piggledy in my memory. But now, it was off to a new world full of dreams and hopes.

I returned to Peine, this time as a free man. To obtain an identity card with my real name on it, I went to the Town Hall to get a copy of my birth certificate. The clerk treated me with impersonal courtesy and issued the document immediately. He even waived the usual fee. . . .

Here and there I encountered a forced smile on the faces of the Peine municipal officials. Of course, they remembered the Perel family, but nobody dared to ask what had happened to them.

With the birth certificate in hand, I told myself: "*Mazel tov*, congratulations! Solly Perel has been born anew."

I had waged a lonely war for survival, separated from my own world, and I had won. Now I had my birth certificate, and with it they had given me back the identity they once took away from me. However, Jupp still lingered; he was precious to me, an exciting part of my life. Yes, I stand by Hitler Youth Jupp. I do not censure him, I do not hate him, I have no charges to bring against him. He did what he had to do. Under the circumstances he could not have behaved differently.

Outside the Town Hall there was a huge sign: "Relief Committee for the Victims of National Socialism." At first I had some reservations about going in to apply. Was I a victim too? I shuddered at the alternative, the thought of putting myself on the side of the Nazis. True, I had lived as free as they did in the splendor of their world. But what about my tormented soul, my sorrow, my silent suffering? What about the parents who were taken from me, the time I had lost, and my damaged future?

A new worry gnawed. What would those who had survived the death camps think of me? Would they consider me an equal? Would I feel at peace with myself in their company? They had suffered and had been humiliated and tortured, and while they stood at the threshold of death, I associated with their murderers and sat glued to the radio, waiting to hear Nazi shouts of victory. What a terrible contradiction. Perhaps the chasm could never be bridged.

These attempts to assess what had happened to me assuaged my painful inner conflict somewhat, but they couldn't resolve it. Finally, I decided that I had also been a victim of persecution and of the fascist tyranny, and I went in to see the committee that was helping the survivors. The office looked like a storeroom. It was stuffed with premium quality food and clothes. The committee had been set up by political prisoners who had come back from concentration camps. They were running it, joined by the remaining local sympathizers of the Social Democrats and Communists.

I introduced myself by my real name and told them my background. "What!?" one man who was working there asked with a smile, "You're little Solly Perel? I remember you. I knew your father very well." Without asking for further proof of my identity or any other explanation, he suggested I select some new clothes. They also prepared a large package of food for me. I picked out a nice shirt, a new suit, and some other items. Two weeks after my liberation I was finally able to take off the HJ uniform and step into a new life. Gradually the significance of my miraculous survival dawned on me. And I was very happy.

The concentration camp survivors on the committee asked me to help with the establishment of other relief offices around the city. I readily agreed. They planned to compile a list of local Nazi criminals and to report them to the special military courts. We also decided to follow up on what had happened to members of the Jewish community of Peine. One bit of news had already reached us: the tragic death of the secretary of the local Communist party, Comrade Kratz. A few days before the end of the war, he and hundreds of Jews and other concentration camp inmates were forced to board an old German ship. It was sunk and all the people aboard drowned.

Just as I was about to leave, promising to come to the next meeting, two Jews who wanted to return to their homes in Romania came in. They had survived Bergen-Belsen. This was the first time I had heard about this camp and of the horrible, frightful things that went on there. They said the camp was near Celle, and I decided to look for my relatives there.

Dressed in my new suit and loaded with packages, I said good-bye to everyone, wishing the Jewish survivors success in their return to life. I threw my black uniform into the first garbage can I saw. It had fulfilled its purpose; I shed no tears over it. But was my double life really over now?

I sauntered happily through the familiar streets of Peine. Not so long ago I had walked on these same sidewalks, hiding my face under my peaked cap and turning aside for fear of being recognized. Now I walked proudly and joyfully, willing to be seen by all. Solomon Perel was alive despite the Nazis' determination to exterminate me. I was in seventh heaven. After several wartime winters, how good it felt to smell the first spring of peace. The aroma of lilies of the valley filled the air. Peine had not been bombed, and if it hadn't been for the military vehicles ceaselessly roaring back and forth, one never would have known that its people had just experienced six years of the bloodiest and most murderous war of all time.

I went over to the Meiners' restaurant. The Nazi emblem that once hung over the door had disappeared. I walked in. The atmosphere seemed different, but the beer and tobacco smell was still there.

I sat down at the same table as before, watching Thea and Clara and listening to the conversations around me. One of the customers said he deplored the many war victims and the terrible price Germany had paid. In his opinion, the biggest war criminal wasn't Hitler at all, but Churchill, because he had refused to join with the Germans to fight the Russians.

I decided not to get involved and not to let statements like that bother me. I was preoccupied with thoughts of times gone by: my childhood, the hot summer days and the dreams I dreamed. The bestiality of the National Socialist racial lunacy had destroyed these dreams. Determined not to become demoralized, I looked again at Thea and Clara, who were young women now. They worked quickly and efficiently. Even at this hour, most of the tables were occupied. That was to be expected. People would always be drinking beer, sometimes to celebrate something joyful, sometimes to ease a sorrow.

I made my way to the gleaming spigot at the bar, and when Clara came over to fill a glass, I said hello. She answered politely but impersonally. After briefly looking at me, she continued to watch the white foam that was settling in the glass. She hadn't recognized me.

I said, "I'm Solly. I've come back to Peine." Surprised, she stopped filling the glass and came around to the front of the counter. Shaking my hand heartily, she said, "Well, well, Solly, it's been ten years since we saw each other." Her face was wreathed in a big smile.

"Not quite," I said. "Not long ago you served me a beer here." She didn't understand, and I promised to explain later.

She told me that her parents had died the year before and her brother Hans had been taken to a prisoner-of-war camp in England. He had been an officer in the Waffen-SS, she said with pride. I had the feeling that her joy at seeing me again was not quite genuine. While we were talking, Thea joined us. Her reaction was even more restrained.

I decided not to stay. It was clear that the "brown-shirt years" had left their mark on both sisters. But I didn't let this disappointing encounter spoil my good mood or dampen my happiness.

Thirty years later I looked up the sisters again to finish telling them the story of my brash visit to the restaurant as a Hitler Youth. I thought they would be sorry that they hadn't recognized Solly in his disguise. But no, they did not respond, did not understand.

As I was leaving the restaurant, a former neighbor, a very old lady, invited me to stay in a room in her apartment. As children we used to call her "the awful old woman with the stick." I accepted her generous offer. The room was neat and comfortable. And after a good night's sleep, I felt a little better. The following day I decided to take the train to Bergen-Belsen.

After eating breakfast with my charming landlady, I left. At the train station I bought a ticket for Celle, the city closest to Bergen-Belsen. The trip took less than an hour.

From far away, the camp looked as though it didn't belong in its environment, a screaming contrast to the surrounding landscape. Outside the camp, green fields and farmhouses surrounded by colorful flowers created a peaceful atmosphere. Had I come to the wrong place? Was it possible that a death camp had been in operation in an area that reflected the rich abundance of creation? But as I got closer my doubts disappeared.

There were rows of barracks on a vast brown, sandy plain. A cloud of dust hung over everything. Many people were walking around, and ambulances and British army vehicles were driving in and out. The crowd carried me along. The liberated prisoners looked grave. After all they had suffered, no spark of joy was visible in their faces. I heard the noise and rumble of tractors. Someone told me that innumerable mass graves were being filled in and leveled.

And then, from the midst of all these people, I heard my name being called in Polish, "Salek, Salek!" Astonished, I turned around and saw the two Zawatzki brothers standing before me. They had been my neighbors in Lodz, one of them my classmate. They were about my age, and looked in somewhat better shape than the other former inmates. I was the first acquaintance they had met since their liberation, and so it was a happy encounter. We shared many childhood memories. When they urged me to stay in the liberated camp for a few days, I gladly accepted. Arm in arm, we walked over to their barracks. There they offered me a cot that had become available after the death of a former prisoner the day before.

During the three days I spent in Bergen-Belsen the stories they told me filled my mind with terrifying images and impressions. I constantly found myself comparing their bitter fate with what I had endured, and I realized how much life had spared me. Now we had a common destiny, and I could join the survivors. We were all in a vacuum—without a home, without parents. None of us knew whether this uncertain situation would change into something more permanent and secure in the foreseeable future. All of us needed a solid foundation that would permit us to recuperate from the past.

After three days I left the camp and returned to Peine, determined to find out more about what had happened to the members of my family. I would also have to go to other camps to search for them. In Peine I received some additional information about my sister and some photographs of her from former friends of hers.

The news that one of the Perel children had come back to Peine, safe and sound, quickly made the rounds. Quite a few people invited me to visit them; some thought I was David, others thought I was Isaac, but they all welcomed me warmly. I declined most of the invitations, visiting only those families who had photographs of my parents. The photographs they gave me I still treasure today.

Out of sheer curiosity I accepted an invitation to a seance where, through "contacts with the spirits of the dead," I was promised information about what had happened to my family. Having never had anything to do with the occult, I was terribly excited as I entered the room to participate in this mysterious rite that had been arranged especially for me. In addition to the "invoker of the spirits," there were eight others, all strangers. The double drapes were pulled closed; it grew dim. Letters of the alphabet, numbers written on pieces of paper, and various cards were lying on a round table. An inverted glass stood in the center. We sat around that table and held hands over the glass.

There was a tense silence. Minutes passed; no one said a word. Then the medium uttered some incomprehensible sounds. I started to become concerned and concentrated on the members of my family. And then something amazing happened: the glass began to quiver, it shook and moved. I wouldn't have believed it if I hadn't seen it. The glass slid in different directions, rose slightly as if it were jumping over obstacles, and then continued its search for "the secrets of the spirits." I watched closely. I was perspiring. When the glass stopped moving, we dropped our arms, and someone drew back the drapes. The evening light streamed into the room. Nobody spoke.

After a while the medium, who looked exhausted, turned to me and said, "One of the members of your family who is very close to you and whose name begins with the letter D is alive. He lives very far away, probably on another continent."

I immediately thought, My brother David is alive. Is that possible? I was shaken but hoped with all my heart that the news was true.

After the seance, I chatted with the other participants, who were all from Peine. They told me that Mrs. Frieden-thal, a Jewish neighbor who had not left her house in town all through the war years, had survived. Her daughter Lotte, an unusually beautiful young woman, had been accused of "racial disgrace" and executed. . . .

Before leaving, I thanked them all for having invited me to such a moving encounter. Wouldn't it be wonderful if the medium's prophecy that my brother was still alive were to turn out to be true?

The next morning I went to see Mrs. Friedenthal. She was happy to see me, seemed to be in good health, and was amazingly sharp mentally. What courage and spirit it took to live anathematized for more than twelve years, under constant threat of death. Yet she had endured in her own home, firm as a rock in a raging sea. It should be noted that Mrs.

Friedenthal had been married to a Christian German who had died many years before.

Mrs. Friedenthal suggested that I stay with her, but I was determined to leave Peine and to go to various concentration camps to try to find my family. I told her to be of good cheer and wished her continued good health. I also promised to come back. She eventually moved to an old-age home in Hanover and died there in 1978 at a ripe old age.

On one of my trips to the camps I met two Soviet officers who were members of a delegation from the Soviet occupation zone, assigned to track down SS killers and to arrest them. I told them in Russian that I was a Jewish refugee and asked them if they would help me get a transit permit to travel to Lodz and Auschwitz in the Russian occupation zone. They promised to try, and asked me in the meantime to serve as their interpreter. Not only was this a challenge, perhaps it would also help me to combat the inner emptiness that followed my uprooting. So I enthusiastically accepted their invitation and went back to Peine to get my things. We drove to Magdeburg in eastern Germany, where the liaison detachment of the Soviet occupation authorities was stationed. Riding in their elegant Mercedes was a pleasure, and I found myself happily humming *Hatikvah*.

"That's a beautiful song, Salomon Azrielowitsch, what is it?" the senior officer, Major Pjotr Platonowitsch Litschman, asked.

"It's the Jewish anthem," I replied proudly.

"I didn't know the Jews have an anthem," he said.

"Oh yes. We even have a flag," I said, recalling the meetings of the Gordonia Club in Lodz and surprised that I hadn't forgotten what I learned there. "The only thing we don't have, Comrade Major, is a country," I added.

Who could have predicted that three years later, in May 1948, the establishment of the State of Israel would be an-

With Soviet Major Litschman, Öbisfelde, 1945.

nounced? I simply could not imagine that the hope expressed in *Hatikvah* would ever become reality.

Registration centers were being set up throughout the
Soviet occupation zone where all German men in a certain
age group had to report and provide information about

themselves. They were also examined to see whether they had their blood type tattooed under their upper arms, an indication that they had been members of the Waffen-SS. Anyone with such a tattoo was arrested on the spot. I was an interpreter in one of these offices. I also translated the conversations of Soviet higher-ups with the Secretaries of the Social Democratic and Communist parties.

The Soviets wanted to unite these two parties and to prepare the way for the founding of the German Democratic Republic in East Germany. In April 1946 the parties were combined to form the Socialist Unity Party (SED).

One of the worst moments in the conversations I interpreted came during a talk Major Litschman had with a high-level representative of the Church shortly before the Nuremberg trials of the Nazi war criminals were to begin. "For Christians," the Church representative said, "the Last Judgment takes place before God. Those who show that they are repentant can expect forgiveness from the All-Merciful." Litschman was indignant with this sort of exculpation. He asked whether God also would justify and forgive the murder of millions of children and babies. The clergyman replied that the children had not suffered by being killed; only the adults had feared death. God intended to punish them for their mistakes and through this penance lead them back onto the right path. After hearing his answer, the Soviets showed the pious man the door.

I hadn't given up the search for my parents and was writing to many people and places to collect any available shreds of information. One of these letters went to a friend of my sister Bertha in Peine. I told her where I was staying and asked her to let me know if any members of my family were to turn up in Peine. After a few weeks I received a reply. She wrote that my brother Isaac and his wife, Mira, had visited Peine not long before. My brother Isaac was alive! I was overjoyed. The letter also said that Isaac had been trans-

ported from the Vilna ghetto to the Dachau concentration
camp. There he was liberated by the Allies and was now living in Munich. I wrote to him immediately, asking him to
visit me as soon as possible. I said I would be able to get him
across the border into the Soviet zone, and was hoping with
all my heart to see him. It wasn't long before I received an
answer. Isaac and Mira were on their way!

We met in the border town of Öbisfelde. It was a profoundly moving and happy moment.—Mama and Papa, can
you hear me? Your blessings and prayers have come true.—
When Isaac told me that our brother David was also alive
and living in Palestine, I wept tears of joy.

Now I also found out what had happened to Bertha. After the Vilna ghetto was disbanded, she and Mira were transported to the women's concentration camp, Stutthof, near
Danzig. In 1944, as the Russian army came closer, the Germans decided to transfer the Stutthof concentration camp
inmates to Ravensbrück. What was later called the Death
March began. It was bitter cold. When Bertha's feet froze,
Mira tried to support her with the last ounce of her strength,
but it turned out to be a desperate and useless rescue attempt. Bertha simply could not go on. She was shot in the
neck by one of the guards. Mira saw the blood flowing from
her open mouth onto the white snow by the side of the road.
Oh God, how terrible it is for me to have to write this. . . .

Later an official car drove us to the Litschmans' villa.
Maria Antonowna Litschman welcomed us. Bottles of wonderful old wine were brought up from the cellar. We emptied them, one after another, in celebration of the survival of
the remainder of our family.

For hours we talked about the past and the present. Isaac
told us about the fighting going on in Palestine against the
British to force them to allow unimpeded Jewish immigration. This information would prove to be very important for
me. A plan was taking shape in my mind. Later, it would

come to fruition very quickly. It was at this meeting with my brother and Mira that I thought for the first time of going to Palestine.

Mira was expecting a child shortly, so they had to go back to Munich. We said good-bye, planning to meet again soon. A few days later I received a card saying that Mira had given birth to a daughter, Naomi.

In the summer of 1947 I was ordered to go to the Soviet headquarters in Berlin-Karlshorst. There, a civilian official received me courteously. He suggested that, since I had made a reputation for myself as an interpreter, I should enter a cadre school in the Soviet Union. He indicated that at the end of my studies I would have an active role working for the Soviet Occupation Authority. I felt uneasy: Did I want to go into another elite boarding school, even though this time I wouldn't have to resort to a double identity and a false name? I just couldn't drum up any enthusiasm for such a prospect, but I promised to think it over, to weigh the pros and cons, and to get back to him as soon as possible.

I went back to my room and, after closing the door, I thought it through. There were two ways to go—to spend a few years in the Soviet Union to prepare myself for a life with an uncertain but promising future. Or to join my surviving brothers and sisters and dedicate myself to building and developing a country of our own where I would feel at home—in Palestine.

The die was quickly cast. No enticement and no force on earth could get in the way of my longing for my family and for a country of my own. I felt I had to set out on my journey immediately.

It took me just two days to take care of some personal things. On my last evening with my friends, we said a sad good-bye to one another.

I had told Alfred, Major Litschman's chauffeur, of my plans, and he picked me up late that evening. We drove toward the border, and he showed me a secret path leading to the West. From there I took the train to Munich and arrived at the city's bombed-out station, which was teeming with people. A taxi took me to Neu Freimann, a suburb surrounded by greenery and full of flower gardens. My heart was pounding when I rang the bell at 18 Sternweg.

My brother opened the door, astonished to see me standing there. We embraced, and after giving Mira a long hug, I walked over to the crib to see the baby. I shall never forget Naomi's smiling little face and her blond curls.

We had dinner together and, to calm their apprehensions, I answered Isaac and Mira's questions, providing them with a straightforward explanation of my plans. It was the first time since I had left my parents that I felt at home with a family, and gradually all the mental tension of the preceding years dropped away. I was getting used to this new life in which I was no longer forced to rely only on myself. Isaac had become a father-substitute, a function he fulfilled until his death. Isaac worked in the editorial offices of *Ibergang*, a Yiddish-language newspaper published in Munich. It was printed in the Roman alphabet. Several members of the editorial staff, survivors of the Dachau concentration camp, used to visit us now and then; they would talk about their dreadful experiences.

I did not participate in these conversations. I only listened, shocked and shaken by what I heard. I felt somewhat ill at ease, as though I didn't quite belong among them, and so I kept my personal burden, my own *Shoah*, to myself. Once, one of the former inmates asked me about my experiences and how I had made it through the war years. I could barely reply to his question. An internal resistance kept me from telling the story. But the little I revealed aroused their curiosity. Most of them didn't believe me, and one man went so far as to brush off what I said, calling it fantasy. I promised to bring them living proof that I was telling the truth. That's when, with Mira's consent, I invited my Munich friend Otto Zagglauer to stop by for coffee.

Toward the end of 1946, an ORT* school opened in Munich, and I registered for a course in precision mechanics. The basic knowledge I had picked up in the specialized workshops of the Volkswagen plant was helpful. I studied there for almost an entire semester.

Then I heard that the *Haganah* was setting up an office to recruit volunteers for the Jewish defense forces in Palestine. I signed up immediately. When I heard the *Haganah* staff people speaking Hebrew to one another, I was very moved even though I couldn't understand a single word. The recruiting formalities were quickly completed, and an early date for my immigration was set. While waiting, I listened to radio news reports of the brave deeds of the Jewish fighters in Palestine. I wanted to participate in that struggle. This time I was not going to be fighting against my will or in the ranks of the enemy. This time I would do it enthusiastically and with conviction for my people, my country, and myself.

I received my travel permit two days after independence was declared in Tel Aviv. As I said good-bye to Isaac, Mira, and little Naomi, whom I loved so very much, I expressed the hope that they would soon follow me.

A large, canvas-covered truck took us to the harbor in Marseilles. After a few weeks in Camp Saint Germaine, we set sail for Haifa on the ship *San Antonio* one dark July night in 1948.

---

* ORT is an organization that worked in displaced persons camps training people in skills and languages that would help them to emigrate.—trans.

In Munich, 1947, before my departure for Israel. (Courtesy of Ehrenfried Weidemann.)

I no longer recall how many days we were at sea, but it seemed an eternity because we were so eager to get to Israel. Conditions aboard ship were rough. Finally, one sunny day, a jubilant shout went up across the dark blue Mediterranean, "Israel in sight!" We embraced one another on deck. My traveling companion Eliahu Beth Josef, who is still my good friend today, threw his arms around me, and we cried with joy.

The ship put ashore near the Haifa harbor, and a truck took us to a military camp at Beth Lid, where we were inducted. After swearing an oath of loyalty to the State of Israel, we were given a forty-eight-hour furlough. I rushed to Tel Aviv to find my brother. The prophecy of the medium in Peine was now fulfilled. How happy I was to see David again! In a corner of a room in his home there was a child's bed on which Azriel, our parents' eldest grandchild, was playing.

David and his wife, Pola, told me about the tragic deaths of our mother and father. Papa had died of starvation and weakness; he was buried in the Jewish cemetery in Lodz. David and Pola had been at the funeral.

In 1989 I visited that cemetery. I was fourteen years old when I had to leave my father, and now at the age of sixty-four I stood at his grave. A sad circle had been closed.

In 1944 Mama and other ghetto residents were forced into an airtight truck. When the truck began to move, the exhaust gases were directed into its interior. The bodies of all those who were killed by this means, including Mama, were then thrown into a mass grave in Chelmo near Lodz.

David and Pola were among the last eight hundred Jews left alive in the Lodz ghetto. After the Red Army liberated the ghetto, they emigrated to Palestine via Italy.

In Leipzig, 1993.

The two days of my leave passed quickly, and I returned to the military camp in Beth Lid. Once we had become somewhat accustomed to the heat and the dry thorny brush, we boarded a bus operated by the Israeli Transit Company, Egged. It took us on the tortuous "Burma Road," as it was called, to occupied Jerusalem. There I served as a soldier in the 68th Regiment of the Jerusalem Division, led by Moshe Dayan.

A new chapter had begun. But this time I would share it with thousands of other immigrants, always remembering what my mother had said to us the last time we saw her:

You must stay alive . . .

Epilogue

You have read my story, and you will have questions— questions that I once feared, that paralyzed me, and that, for a long time, kept me from telling this story. Now I have told it and I have resolved to face all questions openly and honestly.

This has been far more than the originally intended self-therapy. In 1988, when I began to write this book, I had no idea that my story would have such universal impact or that it would have such relevance to the rise of neo-Nazism in Germany. Since then I have spoken with many people about the subject, discussed it and argued with them too. I shall continue to do so, because it's the best way to keep our memories alive. Memory is the most effective bulwark against the "brown," the neo-Nazi threat. I, the Jew Solly, know the Nazi Jupp in me. And I am prepared to confront provocations even from fifteen- and sixteen-year-old youths. For example, recently at a school assembly in Duisburg, Germany, a few boys applauded when I mentioned September 1, 1939, the fateful day Germany invaded Poland. I asked them why they had done that, and then I talked with them. I not only called their attention to the terrible Nazi atrocities and the toll of World War II, which was instigated by the Nazis—the fifty million dead, including the six million murdered Jews and, yes, millions of Germans killed— but I also told them about Jupp. They must learn how they are being led astray, how they are being blinded, and how in the end they will be sacrificed. They must recognize the dangers of these ideologies. I offered these students the greeting *"Shalom"* [peace], and I believe they understood. Today's young people are not responsible for the horrors the Nazis committed, but they *will* be responsible if they ever allow it to happen again.

I had an entirely different encounter during a discussion in which I participated in Berlin. An elegant older gentleman, who had raised his hand several times in an effort to speak, obviously lost his nerve when he was finally recognized. Nevertheless, he stood up hesitantly, a look of great tension on his face. He said he wanted to share with us a secret that had lain buried within him for decades. It was as though the door to a concealed chamber in the depths of his soul had opened. He was Jewish, about my age, and he described how he had survived the Hitler years in Germany. He was hidden from the Nazi executioners in a tiny room in a small apartment in Berlin. With a trembling voice he told us how he had stood behind the window curtains of this room, full of fear and terror, watching the Hitler Youths marching by. The longer he had to stay concealed in this room, confined to a few square feet and without contact with the outside world, the greater became his misery. More and more often, the little Jewish boy would dream of being a Hitler Youth too.

There was a perplexed silence in the hall.

"Because of your candor," the man said to me, "you have made it possible for me to tell my story. I have never before dared to do that. . . ."

In another German city, the usual long line had formed after I read excerpts from this book. People who had listened and who had joined in discussing my story afterwards were waiting for me to sign the copies they had bought. A man about 80 years old had not taken a place in line. From time to time, as I looked up, I saw him patiently standing there, holding a copy of my book. Finally, he said he wanted to talk to me privately. When he was the only one left, he told me, in a low voice, that he had been a high-ranking SS officer. And I had appeared to him that evening like "someone sent by heaven." He said that I had given him an opportunity to ask for forgiveness. But did he really want forgiveness for the crimes of the past, or did he want understanding in this situation? There will never be forgiveness of those crimes, nor should they be forgotten. However, I am not filled with vengeance, and therefore I can respect a confession like this. But, as I explained to the old man, it makes sense only if you break your silence, if you honestly and openly disclose to the younger generation what you did and what you saw. You must describe it, including all its ghastly horrors. I challenge you to stand up and confront the newly sprouting neo-Nazism so that such atrocities will never again be committed in Germany and in the name of the German people.

With this book I offer to make a modest contribution to that goal. In this way, the horror and the madness of my survival will have served an additional purpose.